PUB W[illegible]

IN

Hertfordshire

Alan Charles

COUNTRYSIDE BOOKS
NEWBURY BERKSHIRE

First published 1994

This new edition 2007

COUNTRYSIDE BOOKS
3 Catherine Road
Newbury, Berkshire

To view our complete range of books,
please visit us at
www.countrysidebooks.co.uk

ISBN 978 1 84674 046 6

Cover picture of Aldbury supplied by
Pictures of Britain (Raymond Lea)
Photographs and maps by the author

Designed by Peter Davies, Nautilus Design
Typeset by Jean Cussons Typesetting, Diss, Norfolk
Produced through MRM Associates Ltd., Reading
Printed by Cambridge University Press

Contents

AREA MAP SHOWING LOCATION OF THE WALKS

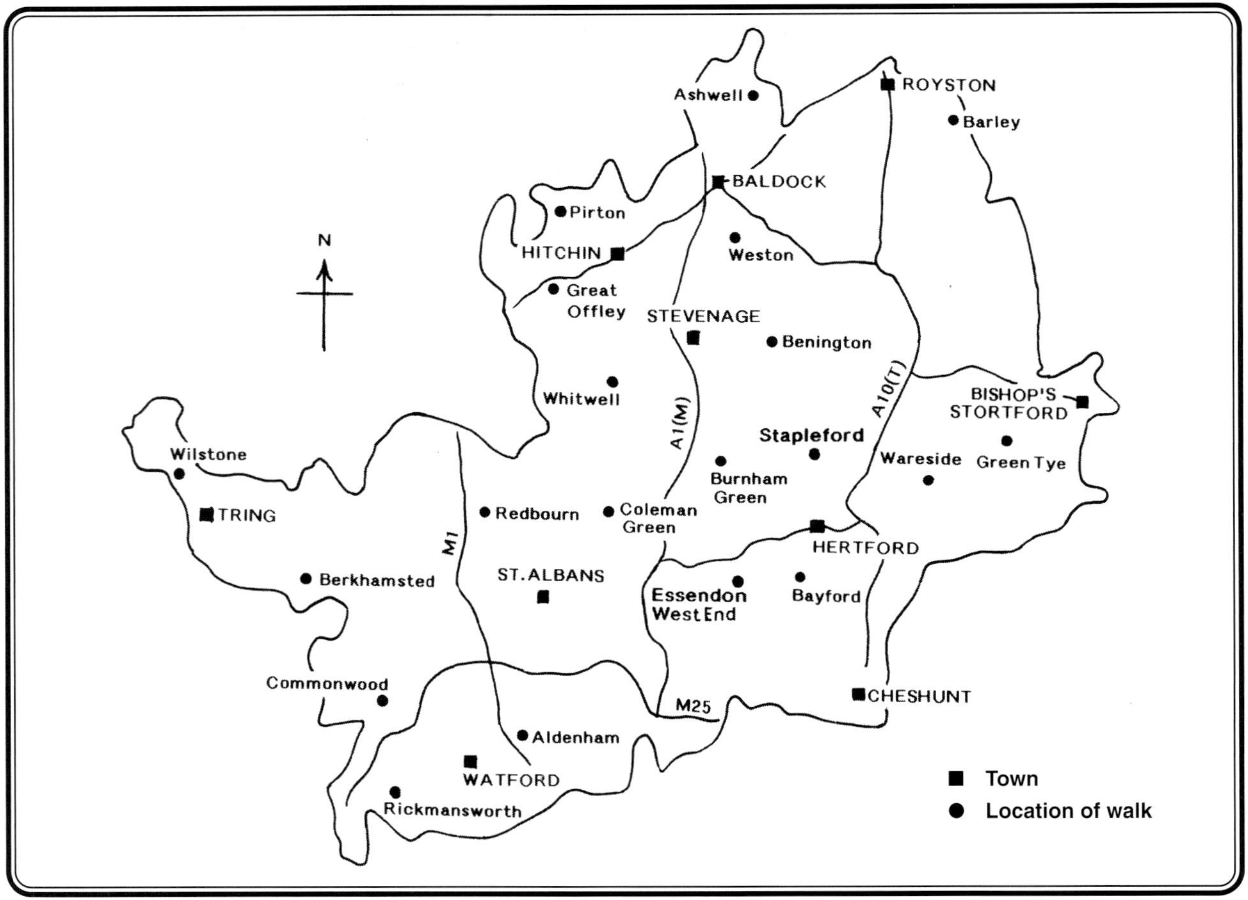

Walk

PUBLISHER'S NOTE

We hope that you obtain considerable enjoyment from this book; great care has been taken in its preparation. However, changes of landlord and actual closures of pubs are sadly not uncommon. Likewise, although at the time of publication all routes followed public rights of way or permitted paths, diversion orders can be made and permissions withdrawn.

We cannot, of course, be held responsible for such diversion orders and any inaccuracies in the text which result from these or any other changes to the routes nor any damage which might result from walkers trespassing on private property. We are anxious though that all details covering the walks are kept up to date and would therefore welcome information from readers which would be relevant to future editions.

The simple sketch maps that accompany the walks in this book are based on notes made by the author whilst checking out the routes on the ground. However, for the benefit of a proper map, we do recommend that you purchase the relevant Ordnance Survey sheet covering your walk. The Ordnance Survey maps are widely available, especially through booksellers and local newsagents.

INTRODUCTION

A glance at a map of Hertfordshire might lead you to the conclusion that this is a county with more than its fair share of major highways, and as such cannot be an area in which to find peace and tranquillity. While this is true in some parts of the county, there remains mile upon mile of delightful countryside where it is possible to 'get away from it all' and, better still, where quiet country walks can be enjoyed. When, as in this book, such walks are based on good country pubs, the walker's pleasure is complete.

The 20 pubs featured here have my seal of approval. Many were recommended by friends and casual acquaintances (my thanks to all of you) while others were discovered by chance. In the main they have been chosen for atmosphere, for quality of food and price (pubs selling expensive bar food have as far as possible been avoided). Not being an expert in the liquid arts I have to confess that the quality of the ales has not figured very largely in my choice. I have simply listed the brews that are on offer.

Many of the walks give access to other (mostly untried) pubs along the way. Where space allows these are shown symbolically on the sketch maps. They could be used as alternatives to the featured pubs – or as additions if it's a hot and thirsty day!

Many pubs are open for drinking during what I have called 'traditional' hours. Give or take half an hour at each end, these are 11.30 am to 2.30 pm and 6.30 pm to 11 pm. I have given actual opening times only when they differ significantly from this. References to 'all day' opening should generally be interpreted as 11 am or 12 noon to 10.30 pm (on Sundays only) or 11 pm.

Lunchtime food is usually available between 12 noon and 2 to 2.30 pm. For evenings a popular 'sitting' is 7 pm to 9 or 9.30 pm. There are numerous variations on this: for example, some pubs serve meals lunchtimes only; many do not serve meals on Sunday evenings, while others serve no food at all on Sundays.

Some licensees are perfectly happy for customers who buy drinks to bring their own food and to eat this in the garden. There are others who merely tolerate the practice, and yet others who are strongly opposed. It is advisable to make absolutely certain before opening your lunchbox, especially if you are in a party all expecting to eat DIY.

Changes in the law relating to children in pubs have enabled licensees to admit those under 14 into their bars. Since conditions will constantly change as more and more pubs are granted the appropriate licence, comments such as 'children can only be taken into the garden' should not be taken as the last word on the subject.

All of the pubs in this book have their own car parks, and all of the licensees are happy for customers to leave their cars while on the walk – but it would be polite to ask first.

The walks average about 4½ miles in length and should take about 2 to 2½ hours to complete. The distances given are as measured from the map and do not allow for the extra ground trodden when walking uphill or downhill. Most of the walks are covered by the 1:50000 Landranger series Ordnance Survey map 166, with the remainder on maps 153, 154, 165, 167 and 176. These maps are invaluable to the walker since they are clearly marked with public rights of way.

Compass bearings are given throughout the text as an aid to navigation. These bearings can be very useful in woodland or where there are no permanent points of reference. Having purchased your compass all you need is a few minutes' practice in using it. Another useful instrument is a walking stick. Since nettles and briars can quickly take over a footpath, this can be a valuable weapon in your defence.

Enjoy the walks; enjoy the pubs!

Alan Charles

The Coach and Horses

This interesting figure of eight walk is almost equally divided between the towpath of the Grand Union Canal from Batchworth and the track bed of the disused Watford to Rickmansworth railway. The top of the '8' is linked by a path crossing Common Moor, a Site of Special Scientific Interest. Model aircraft enthusiasts are allowed to use part of the moor at certain times. If you wish to avoid them (and their noise) walk on Monday or Friday, or on Sunday afternoon. Since there are no hills or stiles, this walk is suitable for pushchairs, but it could be a bumpy ride!

THE COACH AND HORSES is a beautifully refurbished Greene King tenancy pub, attractive inside and out. Apart from the popular and tasty steak and Abbot Ale pie, the selection of main meals changes from day to day. Examples are chicken and mushroom pie, tuna lasagne and spinach and ricotta ravioli in a rich tomato sauce. Lighter meals include sandwiches, salads and jacket potatoes. These, along with the main meals, are available every lunchtime and evening.

Not surprisingly, two of the pub's real ales are from the Greene King brewery – Abbot Ale and IPA. Two guest ales are also available. The pub is open for food and drink all day, every day. Children may join you in the upper level of the pub, in the restaurant, or on one of the two patios.

✆ 01923 772433.

How to get there: The Coach and Horses is situated along the eastern half of the one-way High Street (the half with few shops). If you are driving to the pub, follow the 'Town Centre' signpost from the A412 roundabout adjacent to Rickmansworth Catholic church. There is a frequent train service from London on the Metropolitan line of London Underground. Turn right out of Rickmansworth station and go downhill under the railway into Station Road; then turn left at the bottom into High Street and follow this right through past the shops and the Watersmeet Centre.
Parking: In the pub's own car park. Roadside parking is scarce and expensive.
Length of the walk: 4¼ miles. Map: OS Landranger 176 West London Area and 166 Luton, Hertford and surrounding area (GR 062945).

THE WALK

1 From the Coach and Horses cross High Street to Talbot Road opposite (not the adjacent works road). Be wary of fast traffic as you cross, High Street is one-way. Passing to the left of a public car park, follow Talbot Road over the Town Ditch; then go right with the road alongside the ditch and between numerous handsome cottages. Do not walk the whole length of the road but turn left into a small car park and over another road to Church Street, where you will be facing the church itself.

2 Turn left in Church Street and follow the curve of the road to the A404 roundabout and forward to the Batchworth canal bridge. A flight of steps on the left will lead you down to the Grand Union Canal towpath. The building just here was once the Boat Inn and had two licences, one for road level and one for canal level! Attached to this is the Batchworth Canal Centre – a worthwhile diversion.

Another worthwhile diversion is to have lunch or tea on *Albert*, a narrowboat often moored here on the canal. One of the original fleet of Ovaltine boats, *Albert* was restored from a very derelict condition by enthusiast Chris Collins working single-handed. It is now a restaurant and tour boat.

To stay on the Grand Union towpath you will need to cross the metal bridge (numbered 172) adjacent to the canal centre. This bridge is above the canalised river Chess where it joins the Grand Union. The main flow from the Chess descends a weir and passes behind the centre. Conversion of the river Chess to a canal between Batchworth and Rickmansworth provided a link between the Grand Union and the town's brewery and gasworks. After about 200 yards you will be making a half-left turn along with the canal. The branch flowing from the opposite bank at this point once fed the wheels of Batchworth Mill, now a water company's pumping station.

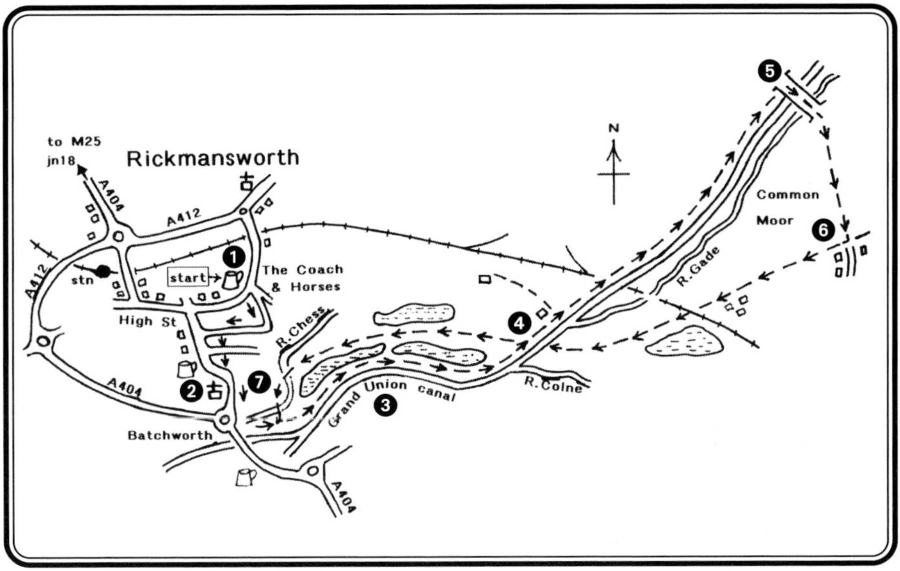

3 In less than ½ mile the extensive waters of Sabey's Pool (a flooded gravel working) makes its appearance through the trees on the left; and soon after this the rivers Colne and Gade join the canal. Having now seen the rivers Chess, Colne and Gade in close proximity you will understand why the local administrative district of Three Rivers is so called.

The steel bridge spanning the canal between the points of entry of the two rivers is included on our return route. It is a remnant of the Watford to Rickmansworth railway which closed to passengers in 1952 and to freight in 1967.

4 You will soon pass Lot Mead House and lock, where a track runs left to the medieval Croxley Tithe Barn, which was restored by the County Council. Another 250 yards will see you under a busy railway bridge carrying trains from London to Amersham and Aylesbury. Beyond the bridge a

stretch of magnificent wild scrub accompanies the towpath. Underneath these plants (much favoured by birds and insects) lie years of rubbish from London's underground stations – replacing gravel extracted for the construction of Wembley Stadium.

5 On arrival at the next lock (⅔ mile from the previous railway bridge), cross both the canal and the river Gade and strike half-right across Common Moor (180°). This will take you in the direction of a distant wooded escarpment (Moor Park Golf Course) and on to the track bed of the former Watford to Rickmansworth railway on the far side of the moor.

6 Turn right in the track bed (there are houses nearby) and commence your 1½-mile walk back to Rickmansworth. In the process you will pass under a railway bridge, then between marshes and lakes before recrossing the canal.

7 Towards the end of that 1½-mile stretch and while walking under tall trees, you will cross an arm of the river Chess followed by the canalised Chess itself. You should ignore a bridge on the left soon after this and go forward to a tarmacked parking area. Turn left here and left again towards – but not across – a drawbridge, and right into a narrow paved path alongside a builder's merchant yard. This will take you to a footbridge and back to the Grand Union Canal.

Go right in the road at the bridge and forward to Church Street. By way of a change you could stay in Church Street and turn right into High Street at the main crossing. Alternatively (retracing your earlier steps, but in reverse) turn right into a rough drive immediately beyond Church Terrace. Soon cross a road to a short path and then right in Talbot Road, following this back to the pub.

THE GRAND UNION CANAL AT POINT ❸ OF THE WALK.

PLACES OF INTEREST NEARBY

Rickmansworth Museum is a short distance from the Coach and Horses and can be visited by turning right out of thc pub and walking as far as the public library, at which point the museum will be in view. It houses an interesting collection of documents, photographs, books and artefacts relating to the history of the area. Opening hours are 2 pm to 4 pm Monday to Friday, 10 am to 4 pm on Saturday. Telephone: 01923 775882.

If you prefer to stay in the open air, you could visit one or more of the **series of lakes** in the area. For this, go under the road bridge from the canal centre at Batchworth and follow the towpath to the first entry point to Bury Lake, the best lake for a first-time visit.

The Cart & Horses

YOU COULD CALL THIS THE 'THREE COMMONS WALK' SINCE IT INCLUDES THE COMMONS AT CHIPPERFIELD, SARRATT AND COMMONWOOD. CHIPPERFIELD, WITH ITS CHURCH, ITS CRICKET PITCH AND ITS THREE PUBS IS CLEARLY THE MOST POPULAR, ESPECIALLY AT WEEKENDS WHEN PLAY IS IN HAND. BY TAKING ADVANTAGE OF A SHORT-CUT (MISSING OUT SARRATT), YOU CAN REDUCE THE DISTANCE WALKED BY ONE MILE.

THE CART & HORSES is situated in a delightful, quiet country corner, and understandably popular with walkers, especially those with a healthy appetite or a demanding thirst. The regular food menu is very extensive indeed, and includes starters, snacks (sandwiches, for example), jacket potatoes and ploughman's. Fish, chicken and steaks come in a variety of permutations under the main meals heading, and vegetarians are well catered for. If you are game for a challenge (and can give 24 hours' notice) you could take on the Ultimate – a gastronomic extravaganza which, along with a 14-ounce sirloin on the bone, includes 54 ounces of meat.

In both summer and winter you can eat here lunchtimes and evenings Monday to Saturday and 12 noon to 8.30 pm on Sunday. Drinking hours are 11 am to 3 pm and 5.30 pm to 11 pm Monday to Saturday and 12 noon to 10.30 pm Sunday. The regular beers are Greene King IPA and Abbot Ale, with Brains S.A. as a guest. Cider drinkers should be equally happy with Addlestone's or Blackthorn.

Well-behaved dogs are welcome inside if kept on a lead. Families are also welcome and, in summer, can make good use of the swings, a climbing frame and a climbing tree. In summer, if you prefer to be outside and it should rain, you can take shelter in the large marquee. On colder days you can stay in this most comfortable of pubs and enjoy the sight and warmth of a real log fire.

✆ 01923 263763.

How to get there: The pub is in Quickmoor Lane midway between Chipperfield and Sarratt. Approach from Red Lion Lane, Sarratt, or from Bucks Hill via Quickmoor Lane.
Parking: In the pub's own car park or in the lanes nearby.
Length of the walk: 3¾ miles. Map: OS Landranger 166 Luton, Hertford and surrounding area (GR 047005). Chiltern Society Footpath Map No. 5.

THE WALK

1 From the pub's car park go along the 'no through road' signposted to Penman's Green. When this road soon turns left go forward through a kissing-gate along a path signposted to Chipperfield Common. This crosses the fields between wire fences (350°) before following a hedge and terminating at a stile by the woodland of Chipperfield

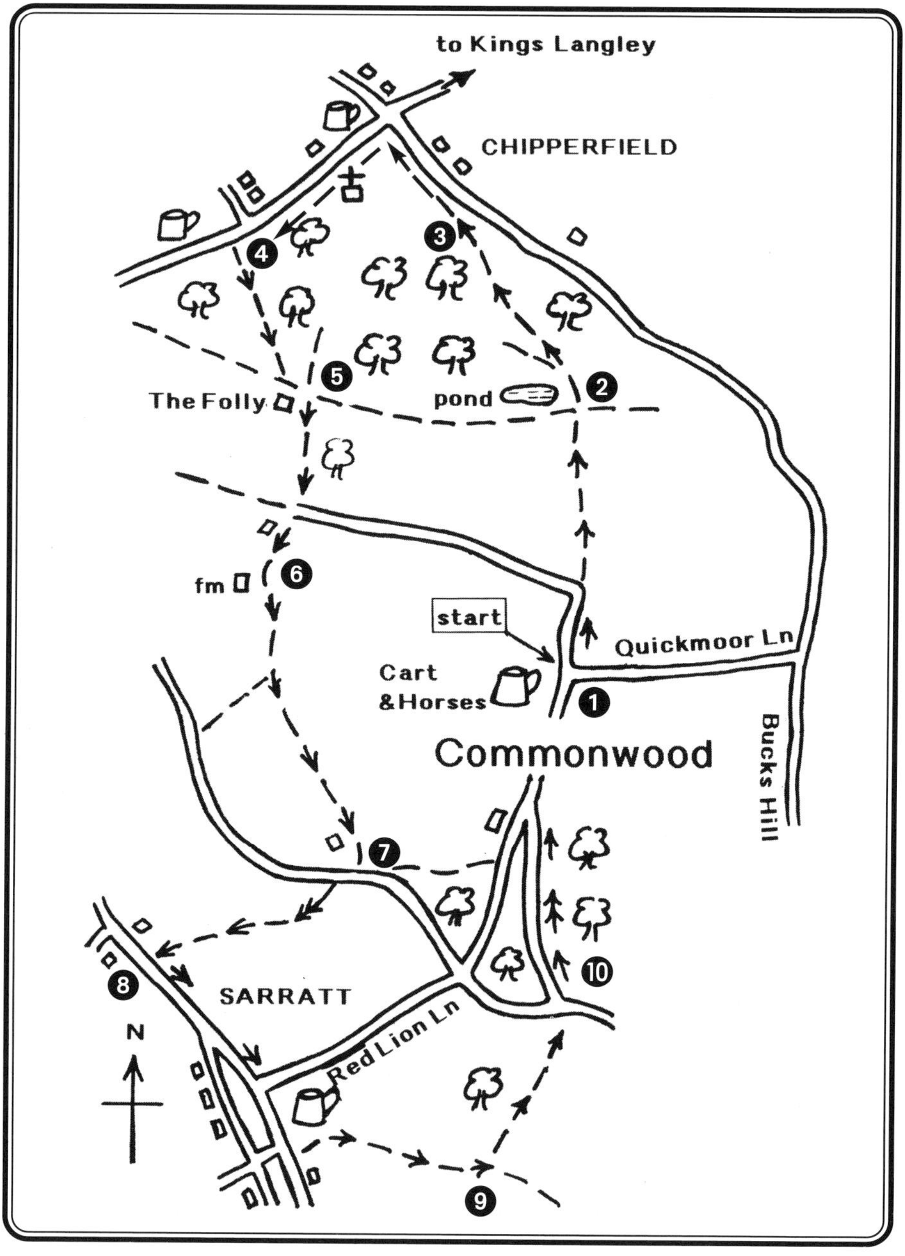
to Kings Langley
CHIPPERFIELD
3
4
5
2
The Folly
pond
6
fm
start
Quickmoor Ln
Cart
&Horses
1
Commonwood
Bucks Hill
7
10
8
SARRATT
Red Lion Ln
N
9

Common. Just ahead of you is one of Chipperfield's best-known attractions, the Apostles Pond. Count the number of old lime trees stationed around its bank and after adding the two that are missing you will know why the pond is so named.

2 Pass to the right of the pond and go forward a few yards to where the main path divides. Take the 'straight on' path, the one with a mound about 100 yards distant (330°). This is a prehistoric burial mound – not a raised platform for archery practice, as I was once told! Veering slightly left from the mound along the wide path between the trees, you will soon have a glimpse of Chipperfield's green. You will also be following a series of waymark posts and passing to the right of one of Chipperfield's venerable sweet chestnut trees. There are about eight of these magnificent specimens in the woods here, each one aged between 400 and 800 years.

3 Having emerged onto the green, you should aim for the war memorial or the Two Brewers hotel. Turn left there and soon pass between the church and the one-time village school (where I spent part of my youth!), now a terrace of three private dwellings.

4 When you are halfway between Queen Street and the Windmill pub, leave the road by turning left from a three-way footpath signpost. Ignore the gravel drive just here – as well as the directions given on the signpost – and cross the grass at right angles to the road; then pass the left side of a stand of gorse bushes. Stay with the path as it veers briefly right behind the gorse (there is a seat here) to a waymark post (No 13). Then continue in the same direction as before (170°) through the wood, ignoring all crossings until you reach a wide bridleway running along the southern border of the wood.

5 All being well you should also come face to face with The Folly, a cottage with a double gateway beside the bridleway. Turn left into the bridleway and go along this for 80 yards, where you will be confronted by a wooden gate ahead. Turn right here to a gap and metal gate. This will place you on a wide path with trees left and a field right. When you meet a crossing of ways go forward along the road signposted 'Private road to Hillmeads Farm' (in fact a public right of way) with Hillmeads Farm Cottage immediately on the right.

6 Passing between the farm buildings go through a kissing gate on the left before reaching the farmhouse, then turn right straight away and resume your former direction. There is a stile very soon which places you along the left edge of a field. Stay with the field edge as it curves left from a cattle trough (160° and ignoring a waymarked path going off to the right) and cross a stile in the far left-hand corner of the field. You will be overlooking an attractive valley as you continue forward and downhill (160°) to the lowest point of the sloping field, where there is a stile, to the left of Dellfield House, which will lead you forward to a rough drive.

7 For a speedy return to the pub (saving one mile) you could bear left from the drive into a signposted path running above Plough Lane, then turn left in the road when you come to a small car park and keep straight on to the pub. For the complete walk turn right in the lane and very soon left over a stile; then uphill in a field along its right-hand edge. After crossing a stile in the field's far right-hand corner you will soon join a tarmac drive which in turn joins the road at Sarratt.

8 Turn left in the road and follow this up to the top of Sarratt Green by the Boot public house. Then turn left into a narrow path just beyond the pub and soon go through a

kissing gate leading into a field. From here the path curves right towards the field's furthest corner (approx 100°), where three other fields abut. Go forward across the fields ahead, aiming for a central kissing gate at the far end to the left of a tennis court.

9 Once there turn left so that the tennis court is behind you, and proceed between a wire fence and a hedge of sorts. From the end of this short path continue forward near the left-hand edge of a field. Tall trees and deep pits over to the left make an impressive sight as you cross a stile and go downhill along the right-hand edge of the next field. Turn left in the lane at the bottom (Bottom Lane) and soon right at a T-junction; then climb the hill for just 75 yards to the first (unsigned) woodland path on the right.

10 Now it's decision time! Either stay on this quiet road to a junction at the top, or follow the path uphill to meet the same junction. For success with the footpath option, you should keep within a few yards of the fields on the right and ignore a stile that appears on that side. While still in sight of the stile (which leads into a field corner), take the second of two adjacent paths on the left. Whichever route you choose – the road or the path – keep forward from the road junction and soon arrive back at the Cart & Horses.

PLACE OF INTEREST NEARBY

Frogmore Mill in Apsley is a unique reincarnation of the tradition of papermaking in the area. A steam-powered paper-making machine operates on certain days, while the mill is open to view on a number of days in each month. From Chipperfield take the road to Kings Langley and turn left in the High Street (A4251) for Apsley. Telephone: 0870 9509272. Web site: www.thepapertrail.org.uk

The Round Bush

THE OBJECTIVE AND CHIEF DELIGHT OF THIS WALK IS THE RIVER COLNE; SO NEAR TO CIVILISATION WITH ITS ROADS, RUNWAYS AND ESTATES, YET SO MUCH APART. THIS ISOLATION IS ALSO ENJOYED BY ALDENHAM VILLAGE NEAR THE START OF THE WALK, BY MUNDEN HOUSE AT THE TURNING POINT AND, TO A LESSER EXTENT, BY THE WELL-KNOWN BLACKBIRD FARM TOWARDS THE END.

THE ROUND BUSH, although technically within the bounds of Aldenham, is in reality in the hamlet with which it shares its name – Round Bush. Having the feel of a true 'local' the pub is obviously very much liked by locals as well as by casual visitors, doubtless on account of its lively but traditional country atmosphere, its good food and its good drink – which includes Abbot Ale, Marston's Pedigree and IPA, with Rosey Nosey and Hobgoblin as guests. The pub is open 12 noon to 11 pm, Monday to Saturday, 12 noon to 10.30 pm on Sunday.

For choice and price the extensive menu will please just about everyone. It ranges from home-made soups and filled jacket potatoes at one end of the spectrum, to appetising main meals at the other, including chilli con carne, fish and vegetarian dishes. Anyone with a healthy capacity can round off the meal with one of the delicious sweets. The full menu is available every day from 12 noon to 2.30 pm (4 pm on Sunday) with extended hours during the summer (weekends until dusk).

Families are very welcome and can avail themselves of the special children's menu. Dogs are allowed in the garden only. Sit with them in summer and enjoy the garden's beauty.

✆ 01923 857165.

How to get there: The pub is a short distance from the B462 1½ miles south-west of Radlett and one mile from the Toby Carvery public house on the A41. It is on the opposite side (south) of the B462 from Aldenham village, in the hamlet of Round Bush. Look for the sign to Aldenham school (*not* Summerhouse Lane nearby).
Parking: In the pub's own car park or along the roadside.
Length of the walk: 4¼ miles. Map: OS Landranger 166 Luton, Hertford and surrounding area (GR 145985).

THE WALK

1 Go right in the road from the Round Bush and soon left in the B462, crossing this to a sidewalk for safety. You will pass the grounds of Edge Grove School before meeting Church Lane on the right. Cross Church Lane to the path opposite and, maintaining the same direction, go along this

between trees to Aldenham's churchyard. After following an old brick wall to its corner keep forward through the churchyard, passing to the left of the church and joining the road in Aldenham village.

2 Turning left along the road and passing to the left of the church, turn left into the drive signposted to Bricket Wood and Wall Hall. The latter is a housing estate on the site of the University of Hertfordshire's former campus. When the drive goes off to the right on its way to Wall Hall, continue forward from a stile and gate along a wide track that runs between trees (hiding a golf course) and fields. Now you must be careful to go through a gap on the left after ¼ mile. This is waymarked with the number 16 and stands near a group of tall Scots pine trees.

3 Follow path 16 more or less straight on under the trees (300°) crossing a number of golf course linking paths in the process. When you eventually meet a tarmac drive turn left and go downhill to Otterspool Lodge. Take a hairpin right turn around the lodge and follow a level path parallel to the river Colne. Passing by an iron gate early on (and in view of a thoughtfully designed pumping station), stay in the path for almost ½ mile to the first crossing.

4 Turn left at the crossing to a footbridge waymarked 12; then over the flat river plain to the river itself and another footbridge. From the second bridge go half-right uphill across the grass, following waymarks numbered 4 (20°) until you meet the tarmac drive to Munden House. Cross the drive to a gravel track and follow this straight on to a stile and gate. From here keep to the right-hand border of a triangular green alongside Munden Home Farm (dated 1880) and turn right, soon passing through a gate numbered 62. From the gate go downhill back to the river Colne – where you have the best view of Munden House.

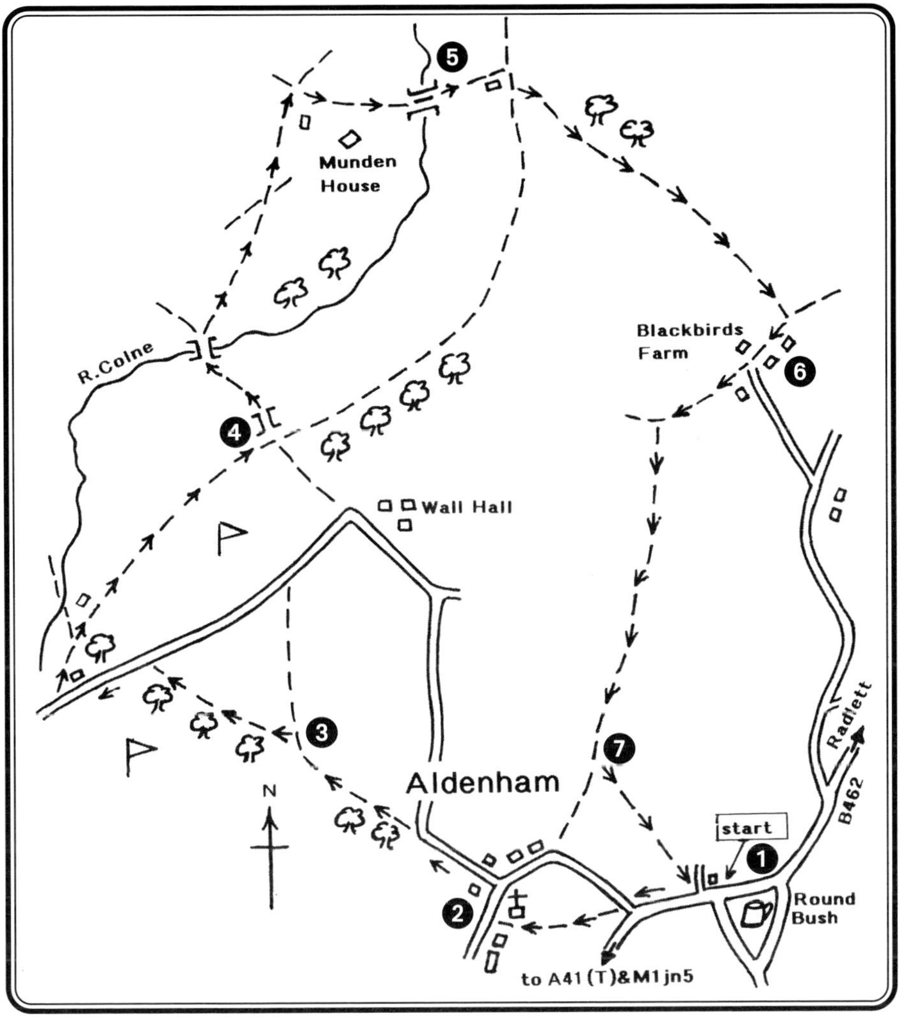

5 The path from the opposite bank of the river will take you along an avenue of lime trees to a gate by River Lodge. Turn right at the T-junction here and soon left into what becomes an uphill meandering track with woodland on the left. You will in due course come within sight (and perhaps smell) of a

sewage farm before the track turns right and enters Blackbirds Farm.

6 Immediately after passing two massive metals barns go through a pair of wide gates on the right and circulate anticlockwise around a concrete farmyard to a track on the far side, guided by waymarks numbered 10. Follow the track downhill between a hedge and a fence and go through a wide gap on the left at the bottom. From the gap go along the left-hand edge of four fields in succession.

7 When you are halfway along the fourth field, and have passed under electricity wires, you should go over a stile on the left and cross a large meadow half-right (assuming your back is to the stile), passing about 50 yards to the right of a pylon (150°). A stile will take you in the same direction across a school sports field to a pedestrian gate adjacent to a school lodge house. This places you on the B462 at Round Bush – close to the Round Bush pub.

PLACE OF INTEREST NEARBY

Aldenham Country Park is a popular area for 'quiet countryside recreation' with 175 acres of woodland, parkland and open water. There are themed guided walks, activities for families and a fascinating collection of rare farm animals. It is open every day of the year. There is an entrance charge for cars, but not for pedestrians or cyclists. The park is signposted from the A41(T) 2½ miles south-east of Aldenham. Telephone: 0208 9539602; it is included in the web site www.hertsdirect.org

The Boat

ALMOST FROM THE START, THIS WALK MAKES A BEELINE FOR THE HEIGHTS OF BERKHAMSTED COMMON. ONCE THERE, IT ENJOYS A TANTALISING MILE OF HEATH AND OPEN WOODLAND. BACK IN BERKHAMSTED THE WALK CONCLUDES WITH ONE MILE OF THE GRAND UNION CANAL TOWPATH.

THE BOAT has a feast of colourful flowers awaiting today's 'boat people' cruising past on a summer's day. Were they to tie up, they could also enjoy a culinary feast, in more than ample proportions and at prices to suit the leanest of pockets. The main meals come as four or five specials chalked on the blackboard, while the old favourites (the sandwiches, ploughman's, omelettes, salads and so on) appear on a regular menu card. Children's portions are available on request. They can enjoy these in the bar area (until 9 pm accompanied by an adult) or on the patio, which overlooks the canal.

In winter, meals are served every lunchtime and evening Monday to Friday and 12 noon to 9 pm weekends. In summer they are available from 12 noon to 9 pm every day. The barbecue is in action every Sunday lunchtime during the summer – outside if it is dry, inside if wet.

The pub is open all day every day throughout the year. Real ales are London Pride and ESB, plus a guest ale changed weekly. There is also a wide selection of wines by the glass.

✆ 01442 877152.

How to get there: The Boat stands beside the canal bridge where Ravens Lane runs into Gravel Path (a road). You can join Ravens Lane from the Baptist church in Berkhamsted High Street. There is a frequent rail service from London (Euston) Monday to Saturday.
Parking: The pub has only a small car park. Roadside parking is possible but limited. Alternative parking is available opposite the castle in Castle Hill, half a mile into the walk.
Length of the walk: 5¼ miles. Map: OS Landranger 165 Aylesbury and Leighton Buzzard (GR 997078).

THE WALK

1 Cross the road from the Boat and go along the canal towpath (canal on your left) as far as the Crystal Palace pub. Join the road here and continue forward towards the railway station. Just prior to the station go under the railway bridge and along Brownlow Road with Berkhamsted Castle ruins on your right. When Brownlow

Road curves right go forward into Castle Hill, and when this turns left, over a stile adjacent to the cricket club drives.

2 The right-hand drive will take you up to one of the club's car parks, from which point you should continue forward but now on grass and roughly following a line of electricity wires in the dip of the fields with a hedge on your left. You will meet a succession of kissing gates before passing to the left of farm buildings. Continue forward in the dip, but now along a track and with a hedge on your right. When the dip curves left beyond a stile, keep straight on uphill to a stile and into a wood.

3 The path climbs steeply through the wood, curving left in a cleared area and meeting a junction of five ways when it is almost at its highest point. Continue forward from the junction, in open woodland, and join a bridleway junction in a small clearing after only 80 yards. Turn left here into what soon becomes a wide bridleway through the wood.

4 After ½ mile of bridleway you will meet a junction of ways centred on a large patch of gravel, with Brick Kiln Cottage and its drive over to your left and an extensive meadow on your right. Branch half-left here (260°) and, passing a private garden gate and fence, follow the meandering path through the trees for a few hundred yards to a private field gate, passing to the immediate right of a massive oak tree at the start and ignoring lesser branches en route. Turn right at the T-junction by the field gate (340°) and walk under the trees parallel to the long field edge until you come to a stile on the left leading into that same field. Go over the stile and follow a succession of right-hand field edges (220°) to a kissing gate to Alpine Meadow Nature Reserve.

5 Go downhill into the dip of the reserve (170°), then straight on up to a kissing gate and out into a field. Turn right and

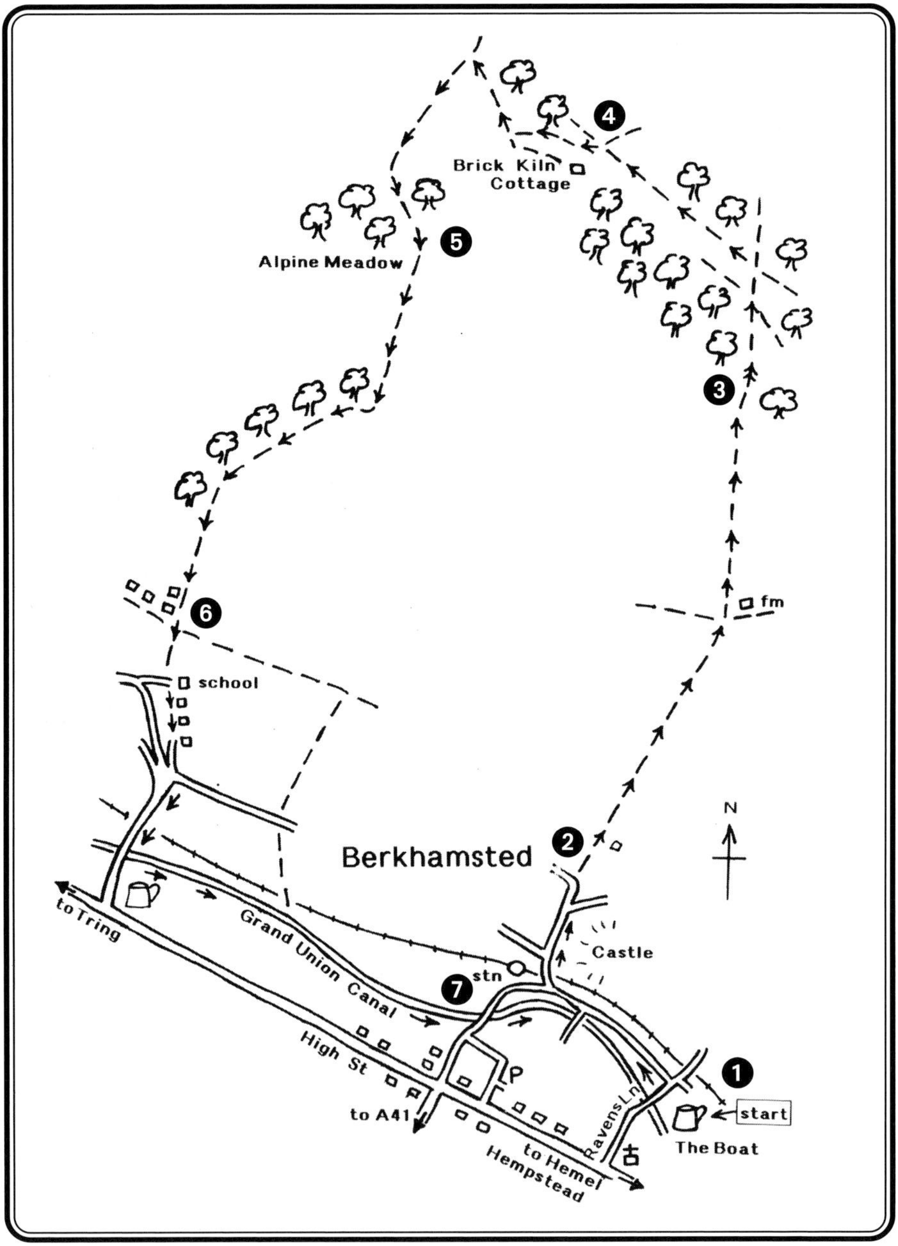

4
Brick Kiln
Cottage
5
Alpine Meadow
3
fm
6
school
N
Berkhamsted
2
Castle
stn
7
to Tring
Grand Union Canal
High St
to A41
to Hemel Hempstead
Ravens Ln
1
start
The Boat

climb steeply with trees on the right to a kissing gate leading into another field. Straight on now, with a hedge on the right, all the way to a woodland corner. Turn right at the corner and follow the long line of trees (260°) as it gradually curves left.

6 You will pass a small pond on the left and a couple of bungalows on the right before reaching a kissing gate in the field's far right-hand corner. Forward now over a crossing and into a path that passes Bridgewater School. Keep to the tarmac path that soon branches left behind gardens and, when it turns left to pass between houses, continue on an unsurfaced path. When the path runs into a drive, follow this straight on down to a road junction. Cross Bridgewater Road (to the left of the junction) and continue downhill over the railway and the canal. Double back to join the canal towpath (effectively turning left from the road) and follow the canal for 1 mile into the heart of Berkhamsted.

7 The railway station (and Castle Hill where you may have left your car) can be accessed via the first (iron) road bridge after ¾ mile of towpath. For the Boat continue to the next road bridge, cross this to the opposite bank (near the Crystal Palace pub) then along the towpath back to the Boat.

PLACE OF INTEREST NEARBY

The remains of **Berkhamsted Castle** lie close to the start of the walk. It is thought that William the Conquerer received the surrender of the Saxons here, following the Battle of Hastings. Entrance is free.
Telephone 01442 871737 (for the key keeper).
Web site: www.berkhamsted-castle.org.uk

The Half Moon

YOUR ENJOYMENT OF THIS WALK MAY WELL ARISE FROM THE TRANQUILLITY AND QUIETNESS THAT IS EVERYWHERE ALONG ITS ROUTE – AS YOU TREAD THE TOWPATH OF THE AYLESBURY CANAL, VIEW THE RUINED CHURCH OF LONG MARSTON AND CROSS LEVEL FIELDS ON YOUR RETURN TO WILSTONE.

THE HALF MOON is an attractive well-kept village pub with a number of very definite pluses, including a dining-room where children may be taken and, equally important, a warm welcome for walkers. In the winter months you can enjoy the warmth and welcoming sight of a real log fire, and in the summer the large garden – where there is a play area for children.

Top of the bill for eating is the steak and kidney pie made to the licensee's own recipe, and (she modestly admits) by her own hand. She is also well pleased with the specially cured Farmhouse Ham. Her Scottish husband is doubtless responsible for the haggis, a true taste of Scotland sent down from Lockerbie. These, among the score of appetising choices, make up a very reasonably priced menu, to say nothing of the ploughman's, jacket potatoes, burgers, sandwiches and the children's menu. Meals are served every lunchtime and evening except Monday evening. Drinking hours are traditional. There is a choice of around three ales which include Adnams Best and Broadside, with Black Sheep as a 'guest'. Draught cider is Blackthorn Dry. Dogs may be brought inside if kept on a lead.

✆ 01442 826410.

How to get there: From the dual A41 roundabout ½ mile west of Tring, follow the B4009 (not the A41) for ½ mile only; then keep ahead for 1 mile to Aston Clinton. Turn right there (Marsworth direction) onto the B489 and left for Wilstone after 1½ miles.
Parking: In the pub's own car park or along the roadside nearby.
Length of the walk: 4¾ miles. Map: OS Landranger 165 Aylesbury and Leighton Buzzard (GR 905141).

THE WALK

1 Turn right on leaving the Half Moon and go along to the village hall. Go right with the road there, then left into a rough drive after a few yards. You will pass a small playground on the left and house number 53 on the right, and soon arrive at the canal. You now have 1½ miles of this peaceful canal, peaceful because it only flows from Marsworth on the Grand Union Canal to Aylesbury, a

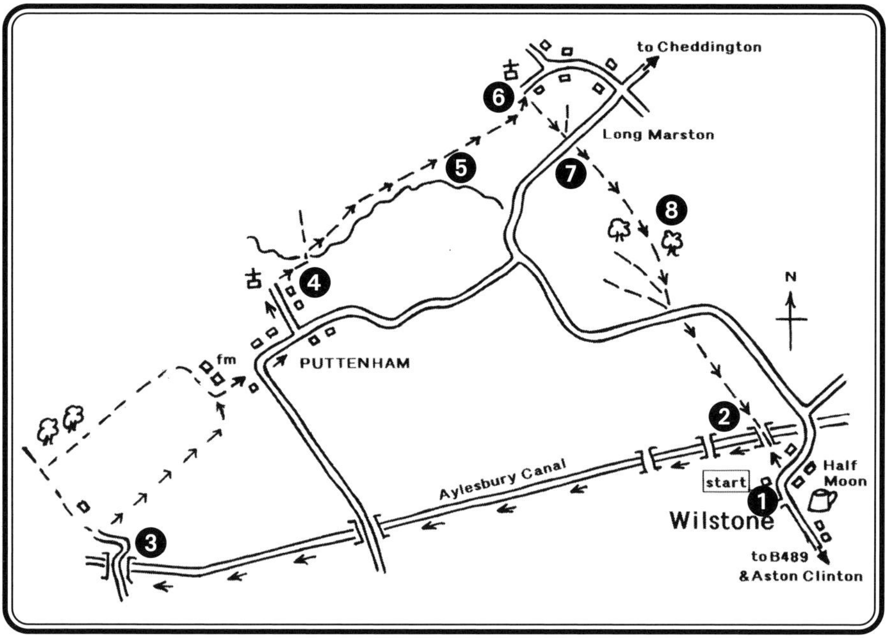

distance of about six miles. The original plan to link this branch to the Oxford Canal at Abingdon came to nothing, and it has seen little traffic since the end of the 19th century. In 1964 plans were afoot to close it altogether. The Aylesbury Canal Society came to the rescue and its future is now secure.

2 Walking left along the towpath you will soon go under two bridges – each carrying footpaths – and a road bridge after ¾ mile. The road bridge is accompanied by a lock cottage. Stay on the towpath for about ½ mile to the next bridge (numbered 8).

3 Cross the bridge and go along the lane, soon turning left with it by Canal Farm. Immediately after the turn, go over a stile on the right and along a path behind farm buildings.

Turn left from the next stile and enter the left-hand field; then turn right and, resuming your previous direction, follow a succession of two right-hand field edges. Turn left out of the furthest field corner and walk parallel to a hedge and ditch, soon meeting a stile and a farm drive. Turn right onto the drive and follow this to the road by Rectory Stables, Puttenham. Go straight on through the village, turning left into a no through road beyond Grange Farm. This leads to St Mary's church with its interesting chequerboard tower of flint and chalk.

4 Go through a kissing gate to the right of the churchyard gate and cross a field (60°) to a pair of gates on opposite banks of a ditch. Walk straight on in the next field for 50 yards to a gated footbridge on the left, and once over this turn right immediately and make for a stile and gate placed centrally at the end of the field. The stile will take you into a very large field, where you should aim for the distant church tower at Long Marston, while keeping parallel to the tree-lined brook on the right (60°).

5 When the brook eventually curves off to the right (taking the field edge with it) you should continue forward aiming to the right of the church (70°) and to a stile in the field's far right-hand corner. If you arrive at the corner of an L-shaped brook under an electricity pole with wire branching three ways, you are in the right place. This should not be confused with an earlier exit at an indent in the field. Continue forward again to a stile in the next field's far right-hand corner, and to another stile almost immediately. From the stile go half-left across a small field to a road by Long Marston's ruined church. The church (only the tower remains) dates back to the 15th century and was demolished around 1880.

6 To continue on the walk re-enter that small field (almost

doubling back) from a footpath signpost near Old Church Cottage. This directs you across the field to a footbridge, which in turn places you in a larger field. Cross this straight on (in line with the footbridge) to a kissing gate on the far side (140°), at a road. As you walk that field you may notice the deep furrows which are reminders of early ploughing methods.

7 Cross the road to the footpath signposted 'Wilstone 1' and follow this between hedges to a gate and along the left-hand edge of a field, then forward across what appears to have once been a tiny field to a gate and ditch, and straight on again to a pair of gates and a ditch in the far right-hand corner of a field. In the next field you should go forward a short distance (30 yards) to a gate on the right leading into scrubby trees. I hope you are still with me in this complexity of gates and ditches.

8 After pursuing the twisting path through the scrub to a footbridge keep more or less straight on alongside a brook and under trees, until you reach a quiet lane. Cross the lane to a gate and go straight on parallel to the left-hand edge of a field (160°). Keep forward in the next, narrow, field to the gate at the far end. Go through the gate into the corner of a sharply angled field, and, cutting off that corner, soon enter the next field. All that remains is to cross this final field to a footbridge over the canal (140°). Wilstone is straight on.

PLACE OF INTEREST NEARBY

Wilstone Reservoir is easily found by turning left out of the Half Moon and right at the T-junction ahead. A small car park lies adjacent to the reservoir. This is a marvellous place to observe wildfowl, especially in winter when many species migrate here.

The Hollybush

I owe the idea for this enjoyable walk to the staff of the Countryside Management Service, who conduct parties along its circular route from the restored Redbournbury Mill. Although the central theme is the much talked about river Ver (on which the mill depends) the walk also enjoys the gentle heights around Hammonds End Farm and the fine old buildings of Redbourn.

THE MILL IS OPEN TO THE PUBLIC ON BANK HOLIDAY WEEKENDS AND OTHER SELECTED WEEKENDS. LIGHT REFRESHMENTS ARE USUALLY AVAILABLE.

THE HOLLYBUSH is a delightful pub in an incomparable setting amongst well-kept cottages and close to Redbourn's parish church. Once inside you can take pleasure in the pub's traditional atmosphere, helped along by the nicely polished brass and copper, by the open fire, and by the licensee's warm welcome.

The menu card at the Hollybush presents an adequate choice of bar meals at reasonable prices. Examples are steak and ale pudding, chicken chasseur and lasagne, with mushroom stroganoff as a popular speciality. On Sunday the menu concentrates on a roast lunch of chicken, lamb or beef, along with a starter and sweet. Food is home-cooked and freshly prepared to order, and is available everyday lunchtimes only (12 noon to 3 pm), with a slightly reduced choice on Saturday. If the absence of food at other times is a drawback you could try the Cricketers not far away across Redbourn Common or the Bull in High Street.

While in winter you can enjoy the warmth of an open fire, in summer you may prefer to be out in the large garden, especially since it won an award in 'Redbourn in Bloom 2006'!

Beers include Foster's, John Smith's and 1664, with Hobgoblin as a guest ale. Opening hours are 12 noon to 11 pm every day (until 10.30 pm on Sunday). Your dog may keep you company if well-behaved of course.

✆ 01582 792423.

How to get there: The pub is near the parish church in Church End, just beyond the south-western extremity of Redbourn Common. Approach from the B487 along Hemel Hempstead Road or Chequer Lane, or from Redbourn's High Street along Fish Street and straight on along South Common. Bus 320 from Harpenden stops on the common nearby and runs hourly Monday to Saturday only. There is a frequent service daily to Harpenden from London on the Thameslink rail service.
Parking: In the pub's own car park or along the roadside adjacent to Redbourn Common. There is also a small car park on the common, near the cricket club and a short distance along the walk.
Length of the walk: 5 miles. Map: OS Landranger 166 Luton, Hertford and surrounding area (GR 101117).

THE WALK

1 From the Hollybush go along Church End towards the common and join a tarmac path just beyond Mymms Cottage. The path crosses the common accompanied by an avenue of trees, and passes to the right of the cricket clubhouse.

2 The tarmac path crosses Lybury Lane and later divides two ways. Take the right-hand branch (straight on) and follow this over another road and between brick walls to Redbourn's High Street. Looking left along the High Street you will see the Bull public house, an important staging-post in times past. It was one of 18 hostelries that existed here when Redbourn was on a main highway (Watling Street) to the north.

3 Cross to Waterend Lane opposite and follow it straight on when it changes to a rough drive, staying with this when it

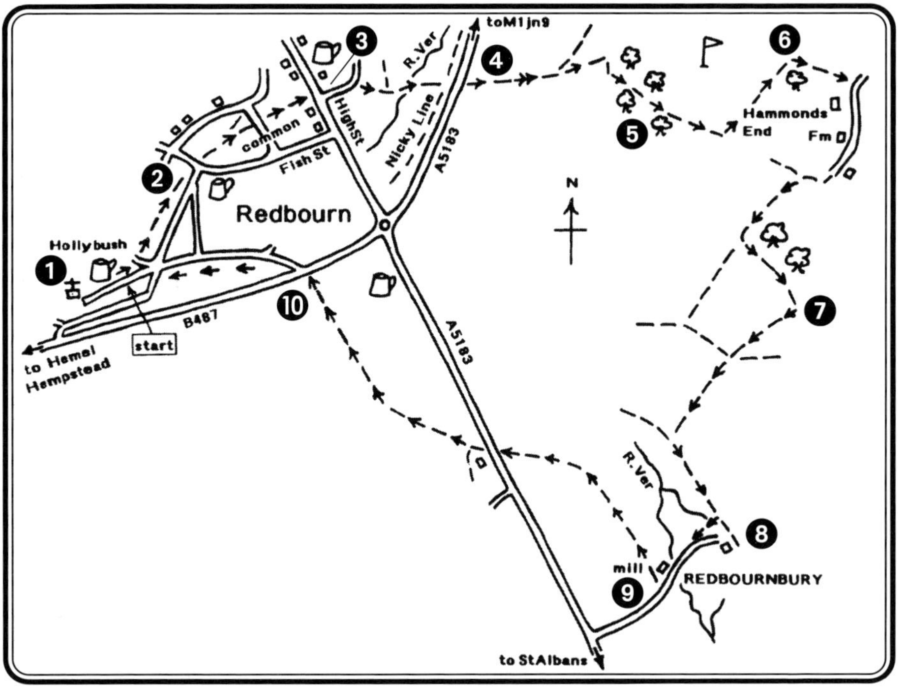

crosses the river Ver at a ford. After passing an abandoned nursery go uphill on a narrow path to the Nicky Line and Redbourn's bypass. The Nicky Line is the trackbed of the former Hemel Hempsted to Harpenden railway. It is managed as a wildlife habitat and is used by walkers and cyclists.

4 Cross the bypass (with great care) to a flight of steps opposite. From the top of the flight walk slightly left (about 70°) and uphill across a field, following a line of overhead wires. This will take you into another field at the top, at its corner. Ignore the path going half-left across the field and continue forward, following the right-hand hedge (still 70°) until you come face to face with an area of scrub. This is about ⅓ of the way along the field that you are now in. Turn

right here with the waymark arrow (180°) then left into the scrub after only 20 yards.

5 As you make your way along the well-used path through the scrub (150°) your view through the trees is of the Ver valley on one side and a golf course on the other. The path comes out into the open at a corner of the golf course, where there is a water tap for thirsty golfers. Pass to the right of the tap and turn left from the corner, then follow the hedge (60°) until you reach another area of hawthorn scrub. Turning right into the scrub (along with the waymark arrow) you will view a further part of the golf course left and a field right, and very soon the lovely three-storied Hammonds End House.

6 Stay with the adjacent wire fence as it curves right to a kissing-gate, and shortly to another gate at a tarmacked farm drive. Turning right in the drive you will pass a preserved pond before going through the farmyard. Follow the drive as it passes a barn and becomes a track. Turn right with it and soon left (ignoring a branch going straight on along a field edge) eventually following a short wood edge (240°) on the left. You should turn left when you reach the corner of the wood (not straight on across the fields) and follow a long wood edge (the same wood) downhill.

7 When you are almost at the bottom, turn right and follow the dip of the fields, with a hedge first on the left then on the right, ignoring branching footpaths as you go. This will take you down to a fishery, which was once a watercress farm. Go left in the track just here and follow this to a ford and footbridge over the river Ver. The Ver has suffered badly over a number of years, much of it being totally dry due to drought and excessive extraction. Thanks to the concerted efforts of the Ver Valley Society, this part of the river flows again in all its beauty.

8 Once across the water (a right-hand turn) soon cross another footbridge and make your way forward to Redbournbury Mill. Although there was a mill here at the time of the Domesday Book (1086), much of the present building dates from 1790 – except those parts rebuilt after a fire in 1987. This privately owned mill is supported by English Heritage and is open to the public on selected days throughout the year.

9 Turn right and join a path immediately to the left of the mill and shortly go through two kissing-gates leading into a field. Follow the field edge, with a hedge on the right, for ½ mile to the A5183. Cross the road to Dolittle Cottage opposite and, passing to the right of the cottage, soon (30 yards) join a fenced path on the right from a kissing-gate, and walk alongside a field. Stay with the path to its far end adjacent to the field corner; then keep straight on, but now along the right-hand edge of a field, to Redbourn's bypass.

10 Cross the bypass to Chequer Lane and stay with this as far as the common, then forward into Church End and the Hollybush. With your observant eye and you will have noticed, at the entrance to Church End, the oldest house in Redbourn, the Jolly Gardener. Also, beyond the pub, an inscription on a one-time workhouse.

PLACE OF INTEREST NEARBY

St Albans City, 5 miles south-east of Redbourn along the A5183, has a wealth of interest including the Abbey (and its excellent refectory), Verulamium Park and Museum, and the Roman Amphitheatre. St Albans was an important town in the days of the Roman Empire.

The John Bunyan

SOON AFTER LEAVING THE JOHN BUNYAN THIS WALK LAUNCHES INTO A MARVELLOUS SUNKEN TRACK AND TAKES YOU ALL THE WAY DOWN TO BROCKET PARK IN THE VALLEY OF THE RIVER LEA. THE PARK, WITH ITS FINE HALL AND LAKE, IS A SIGHT TO BEHOLD, WELL WORTH THE GENTLE EFFORT THAT IS THEN REQUIRED FOR THE RETURN JOURNEY.

THE JOHN BUNYAN PUB, on a quiet country lane and with an outlook across fields and trees, is a great place to be on a summer's day; and in winter the warm glow of the log fire makes it a welcome retreat from the cold. It goes without saying that the pub is named after the author of *The Pilgrim's Progress*, but more of that as we set off on the walk.

There is a good variety of meat and fish dishes to choose from, including that regular favourite, home-cooked ham, egg and chips. Vegetarians are catered for, as are those who prefer filled jacket potatoes, sandwiches, ploughman's or soup. With the beams and walls occupied by 700 or so jugs and plates, you may fail to notice the framed Clean Food Award and Cellar Award certificates. The latter should give you assurance that the real ale – McMullen's Country Best Bitter and Original AK – is well kept. Seasonal guest beers are available all year round.

Meals can be enjoyed every lunchtime and evening except Sunday evenings. Drinking hours are traditional except at weekends in summer when the pub is open all day. Your dog may join you in this two-bar pub, but your children (if under 14) may not.

✆ 01582 832037.

How to get there: Coleman Green is ¾ mile south-east of Wheathampstead as the crow flies, and lies on Coleman Green Lane (mapped as a Roman road). If driving north from St Albans along the B651, branch right into Coleman Green Lane just beyond Sandridge and, keeping left at the first junction, drive straight on for 1½ miles.
Parking: In the pub's own car park or off the lane nearby.
Length of the walk: 4½ miles. Map: OS Landranger 166 Luton, Hertford and surrounding area (GR 190126).

THE WALK

1 Go left along the lane from the John Bunyan and soon leave this for a byway on the right almost opposite a terrace of tall houses dated 1877. The faded plaque on the sad cottage ruin just here leaves us in no doubt why this remnant has

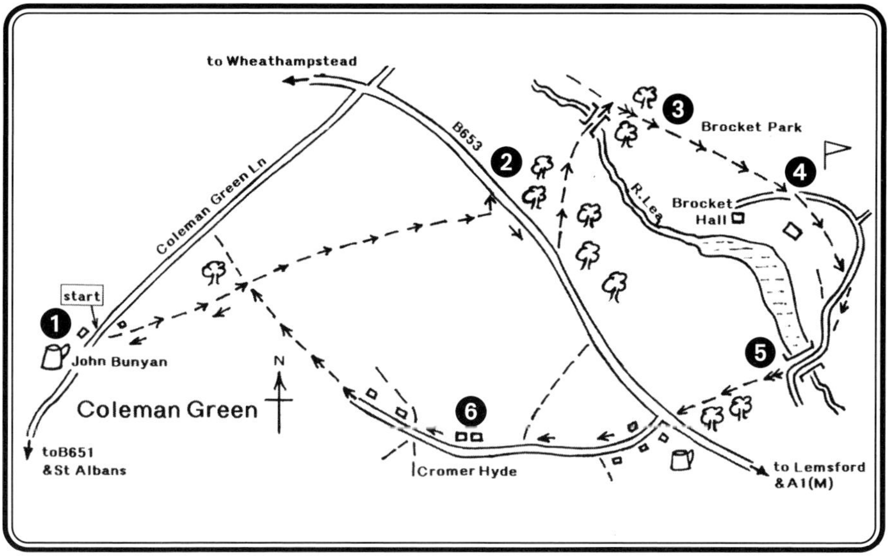

been retained and fenced – and why the John Bunyan pub was so named:

John Bunyan is said by tradition to have preached and occasionally to have lodged in the cottage of which this chimney was a part.

You now have a straight mile of track, mostly hedge-lined and sunken, all the way down to the B653 by Brocket Park. Legally this track is a 'byway open to all traffic'. In practice wheeled traffic might find it difficult, which is fortunate as far as we are concerned. Before the halfway point you will go over a crossing; and when you are in close proximity of the B653 the track (more akin to a path at this point) makes a sharp left-hand turn and goes up to meet the road.

2 Turn right in the road (cross over for safety) and walk the short distance to a gap on the left – halfway along a parking

layby. Here a notice announces Brocket Estate which is crossed by a number of pubic rights of way.

The well-used path through the trees soon widens and drops down to the river Lea. At a crossing 50 yards beyond the river (there is a private gate directly ahead) a waymark post is our next point of reference. Turn right here and climb the short steep slope under the trees, following the waymark posts and a wire fence to a stile and gate ahead.

3 Continue forward from the stile, in line with the waymarks but now across a golf course.

You will soon be following a wooden fence and enjoying a good view of Brocket Hall and its lake. Built between 1760 and 1780 the hall has been home to two prime ministers – Lord Palmerston and Lord Melbourne. It now functions as a conference centre and offers facilities for private entertainment and dining. The park was laid out by 'Capability' Brown. Whether he would have approved of the golf, I am not sure.

4 An overgrown U-shaped pit and a large fenced gas cylinder ('Capability' would not have approved) marks the conclusion of that long fence. Here a waymark beckons you half-right across a drive and into a fenced path, which in turns meets another drive at a crossing. A right turn in the drive (the right of way is actually on the grass alongside) will take you past the main entrance gate and down to the river bridge, where you have the classic view of Brocket Hall and its lake.

5 Leave the drive by continuing straight on from the bridge, climbing the waymarked grassy slope (260°) to meet a wood edge at the top. Keeping to the right of the trees stay with them until you are back at the B653. Left from this point is the Crooked Chimney Pub, with a name that needs no explanation. Cross to Cromer Hyde Lane, the no through

road opposite, and go along this between a number of desirable cottages and forward into open country.

6 The lane continues for a further ½ mile, with more cottages to delight the eye (especially 12 and 14) and various paths leading from the left and right. When adjacent to a farmhouse and its pond, the lane changes to a track and ascends to a high point, giving extensive views across country, including the Lea valley down on the right.

When you have gone straight on over this high point (such as it is) and descended to a dip, you will recognise the sunken path that characterised the start of the walk. All that remains is to turn left in this and make your way back to the John Bunyan.

PLACES OF INTEREST NEARBY

Wheathampstead is an attractive little town on the river Lea, 1½ miles north-west of Coleman Green. To the south of Wheathampstead lies Normansland Common, a pleasant, largely open, heathland. A car park is provided ¼ mile off the B651.

The Candlestick

AFTER DESCENDING THE LEA VALLEY SLOPE ALONG A QUIET LANE, THE WALK FOLLOWS THE RIVER LEA FOR PART OF ITS COURSE. LEAVING THE RIVER IT HEADS FOR THE ELEVATED HEIGHTS OF ESSENDON. FROM THIS ATTRACTIVE VILLAGE IT DIPS INTO LOVELY VALLEY FIELDS AND RETURNS TO WEST END AND THE CANDLESTICK.

At **THE CANDLESTICK**, the story is told that, in an earlier pub on this spot, the bar was lit by a single candle. When it was necessary to bring up ale from the cellar the landlord would light his way with the same candle, leaving his customers in the dark! This is remembered in the name of the present pub and in the many and various candlesticks that decorate the bars.

At lunchtimes and evenings every day (except Sunday evening) there is a good choice of straightforward English pub food with an emphasis on home-made pies. Fish is also on the menu, but if this isn't to your liking you could settle for ham, sausage, fried egg or soup. Cold food includes sandwiches (ordinary, toasted or door-stepped!), salads and ploughman's. You could make a day of it by ending with spotted dick, treacle pudding or apple pie.

Real ales are McMullen's AK and Country Bitter, with other brews being introduced monthly. Traditional drinking hours are kept from Monday to Saturday (closed only from 4 pm to 6 pm on Saturday) while on Sunday the pub is open from midday to 5 pm in winter, 10.30 pm in summer.

Children are welcome at lunchtimes. Although the garden is close to the road they can safely be taken there: this is a quiet corner of Hertfordshire, with very little traffic. Dogs may be taken into the public bar or the garden.

✆ 01707 261322.

How to get there: The pub is in a quiet lane at West End, ¾ mile from the B158 at Essendon. Approach from Essendon along West End Lane. Essendon itself is signposted where the B1455 leaves the A414 midway between Hertford and Hatfield. Turn right from the B1455 into the B158 after ½ mile.
Parking: In the pub's car park or alongside the lane opposite; alternatively just around the corner in the Essendon direction.
Length of the walk: 4 miles. Map: OS Landranger 166 Luton, Hertford and surrounding area (GR 263083).

THE WALK

1 On leaving the pub walk a few yards uphill and turn left at a T-junction into a no through road. Go along this for ¼ mile,

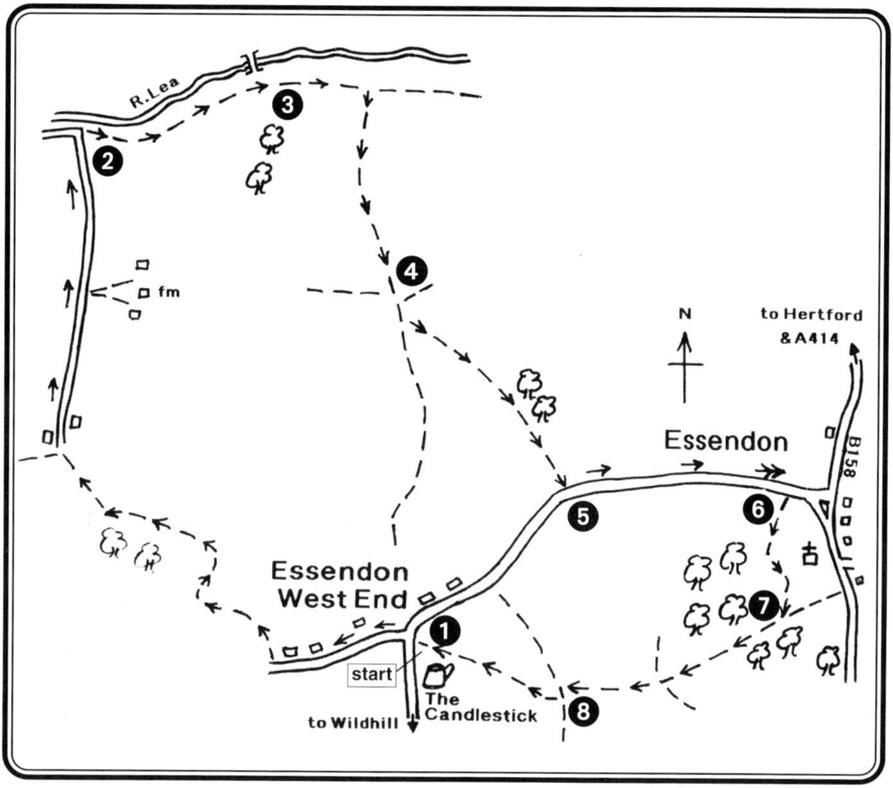

passing Flint Farmhouse on the way. When confronted by a 'private' metal gate, turn right into a track just beyond an attractive semi-detached house. Passing a pond on the left at the start, follow the meandering track for ¾ mile until you meet more houses lower down. The track becomes a tarmac road at this point and takes you all the way down to the river Lea, which is hidden by trees near a sharp left turn in the road.

2 Leave the road here by turning right into a bridleway, which is part of the Lea Valley Walk, a 50-mile route along the

river Lea from its source at Luton to the river Thames in London. We use ½ mile of this path by following the river alongside its shield of trees.

3 Soon after passing (not crossing) a wide river bridge, enter a field ahead and follow its right-hand edge, making your exit through a gap at the far end. Do not go forward into the next field, but turn right into a wide track that climbs gently between hedges and trees.

4 After ⅓ mile you will pass a track which leaves from the right and heads towards farm buildings, and soon after this another which enters fields on the left. Do not go into either of these but continue forward for 25 yards only, while looking for a waymark post in the hedge on the left. Strike across the field half-right (assuming your back is to the hedge), and aim for the distant woodland (130°). This should take you to a waymarked hedge gap 50 yards to the right of the field's far corner.

Continue in the same direction in the next field, cutting off a large field corner and meeting the wood edge by a waymark post. Turn half-right here and follow the wood edge until it terminates; then continue – but slightly right – across the field to the right-hand end of a wide hedge gap.

5 This will place you on the Essendon road, and a left turn followed by a hill climb will take you into Essendon itself.

Before turning right into a level fenced path near the top of the hill (opposite The Little House), why not take a short stroll around the village? Notice in particular an inscription on the south-facing wall of the parish church. This commemorates the rebuilding of part of the church after it was bombed by a German Zeppelin airship in 1916. Cottages nearby were also damaged and two villagers lost their lives, a fate shared by the crew of the 'Zeppy' when it was brought down 4 miles away at Cuffley. While you are in the village, you could also call into the welcoming Rose and Crown for a refresher! This is in the High Street (the B158) along to the right.

6 Back at the fenced path, follow this alongside what was once the well-known Salisbury Crest pub to a gate by the churchyard. Cross the meadow here half-left (210°) to a kissing-gate in the far left-hand corner, then go a few steps forward to another kissing-gate and into another meadow, ignoring a farm gate on the left adjacent to the two kissing-gates.

Follow the left-hand edge of the second meadow to a kissing gate; then cross yet another meadow half-right, aiming for a kissing-gate behind a fenced pit on the opposite side (190°).

7 Beyond the gate turn right and follow a path straight on downhill. This will take you in and out of a wood to a footbridge at the bottom of the valley. Continue forward and uphill along a field edge to a kissing-gate at the top.

8 Go through the gate and turn left into a tree-shaded bridleway, then right from a waymark post after a few yards. Soon pass through another gate and into the light of day. Keep forward here and follow two right-hand field edges (as near as the vegetation permits) to the garden of the Candlestick.

The Baker Arms

A WALK CONTAINING MUCH THAT IS TYPICAL OF HERTFORDSHIRE: GENTLY UNDULATING COUNTRYSIDE WITH SCATTERED WOODLAND; CULTIVATED FIELDS AND MEANDERING BROOKS; NOBLE HOUSES, HUMBLE COTTAGES AND BEAUTIFUL WELL-KEPT CHURCHES. SO MUCH IN SO FEW MILES!

THE BAKER ARMS is one of the gems of Hertfordshire. And if you enjoy good food (and are happiest when you are not paying the earth) you will want to return again and again.

There are three menus: the lunchtime menu, the blackboard menu, and (where you will pay just a little more) the evening menu. All the food on the blackboard menu is home cooked. There are so many items to choose from that you are really spoilt for choice.

Both the young and the old are catered for. Your children may join you inside for a meal and on Tuesday lunchtime granny and grandpa can feast on a 'Pensioner's Special'. Fido is not forgotten either but I'm afraid he can only be taken into the garden. This is a McMullen's pub, so it follows that McMullen's real ale – Original AK and Country Best Bitter – is on sale, together with their Special Reserve. The pub is open all day, every day, while food is served at lunchtimes and evenings on Tuesday to Friday (i.e. no food on Mondays); 12 noon to 9.30 pm on Saturday; and 12 noon to 5.30 pm on Sunday.

Before moving off to the next pub and the next walk you could spend the night at the Baker Arm, in one of the four quality en suite bedrooms.

✆ 01992 511235.

How to get there: If coming from nearby Hertford turn left into Bayford Lane from the B158 about 200 yards beyond the entrance to the University of Hertfordshire Science Centre. The pub is 1½ miles along Bayford Lane. Bayford railway station is ⅓ mile from the pub. Turn right as you come out of the station. Trains run from London (Moorgate) three times every hour, Monday to Friday. On Saturdays and Sundays they run half-hourly from Kings Cross.

Parking: In the pub's own car park or along the roadside nearby.

Length of the walk: 4½ miles. Map: OS Landranger 166 Luton, Hertford and surrounding area (GR 311084).

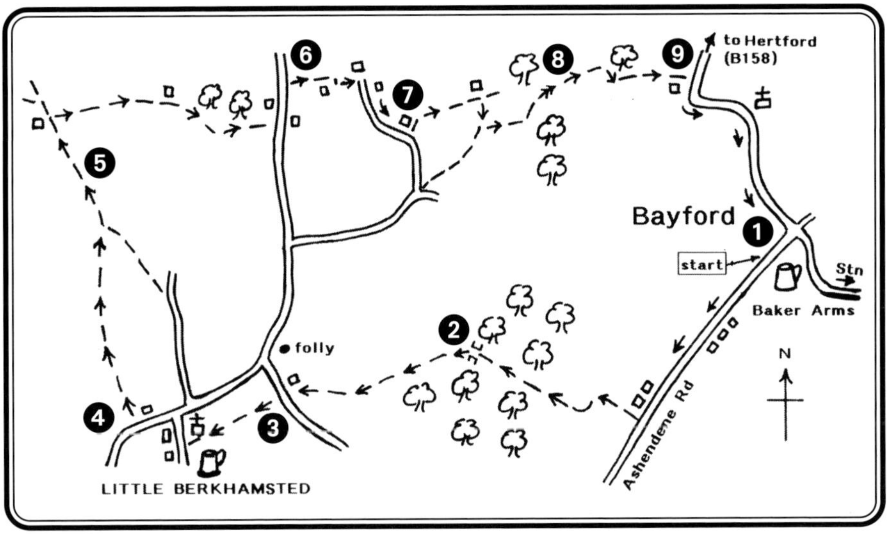

THE WALK

1 Walking left from the Baker Arms along Ashendene Road you will pass an old cottage dated 1640 but now well and truly hidden from view. A quarter-mile further along a pair of semis on the right (Nos 46 and 48) are also dated – 1957. Join a track (signposted as a footpath) just after No 48 and, when it runs into a field after 150 yards, turn left into the footpath proper. This soon meets a stile and places you along the right-hand edge of a field (210° at first). Stay with the hedge as it turns right and leads you to a stile under trees (300°). From here a woodland path crosses a track after 50 yards (ignore a branch over to the right) and describes a mini S-bend. It then runs downhill to a footbridge over a brook.

2 From the footbridge go half-left (250°) and uphill in a field to a stile and metal gate and then in the same direction in the next field to another stile and gate. Bear right to follow a

hedge up to yet another stile and gate, in sight of Stratton's Folly. Built in 1789 this tower is said to have functioned as a terrestrial observatory for viewing shipping along the river Thames! From here a hedge-lined path takes you to the road by Garden Cottage.

3 Turn right in the road and left over a stile after a few yards; then along the right-hand edge of two fields in succession to Church Road, Little Berkhamsted. The well cared for church of St Andrew is here, also an attractive terrace of timber-clad cottages. Turn right in the road and left at the war memorial; then right after 75 yards into a bridleway signposted 'Hertford Road 1½' by Lavender Cottage.

4 A short gravel drive is soon left behind as you go forward through a gate into a field, where a fine view across the Lea valley awaits you. Continue forward, but now between a fenced field and the trees. When adjacent to the field's lowest corner, a path comes in from the right and a signpost directs you over a footbridge (Howe Green) into a narrow bridleway.

5 Assuming you are keeping to the bridleway, follow this for ¼ mile until you see barns and a bungalow on the left, then go over a stile on the right a few yards before the bridleway bears left. This will place you in a field with the bungalow behind you. As you cross the field (80°) you will see Stratton's Folly once again on the hilltop to your right. After walking up and over the field you will find yourself on a grassy track and passing a timber-clad house on your left. Keeping forward in what soon becomes a rough drive you will arrive at a road opposite High Oaks, with a tennis court nearby.

6 Turn left in the road and soon right (100 yards) into a tarmac drive signposted 'Bayford 1', passing a pumping

ST ANDREW'S CHURCH, LITTLE BERKHAMSTED.

station at the start. Leave the drive when it runs into a private garden and go forward along a field edge to a stile. Follow a narrow path first right then left and through to another stile after 80 yards. From here a tarmac drive takes you right and becomes a lane by Little Stockings.

7 Just beyond the well-manicured lawns of a large bungalow and where the lane goes off to the right, join the bridleway to Waterhall on the left, so that the bungalow remains on the left. This soon curves right and uphill between the fields and trees, passes a pond and a tennis court and comes out at a crossing near a collection of one-time farm buildings. Turn right here along a gravel drive and left over a stile (for Bayford) after 100 yards. Keep to the left-hand edge of a field to its bottom left-hand corner (80°) where there is a

pedestrian gate and stile under power lines. Once through to the adjacent field cut across its corner (30°) for about 50 yards to a footbridge under trees.

8 Cross a footbridge under the trees and ignore all paths except the one with a seat and a flight of steps. These steps will take you straight on uphill to a stile and into the open. Keeping close to the trees at the start, cross the field there (70°) straight on and further uphill to its far side, where there is a three-way signpost. Turn right and follow a hedge (140°) to its end; then go between fences across fields, aiming for a cottage (Ash Spinney) on the opposite side (90°). Bayford church will be in view slightly right as you proceed.

9 All being well you will pass along a short path to the left of the cottage. Turn right in the road here and follow it past the church and back to the Baker Arms. If you have time and inclination, do call in at the church and see the board giving 'fees to be taken by the minister, clerk and sexton' for services rendered at baptisms, weddings and funerals. You will also see a number of memorials to members of the Baker family, a name which lives on in today's pub. In the churchyard can be found the grave of William Yarrell, a notable 19th century naturalist. This is within a railed enclosure containing other members of the Yarrell family.

PLACES OF INTEREST NEARBY

Paradise Wildlife Park, a popular attraction for families, is situated in White Stubbs Lane, 3 miles south-east of Bayford. It can be approached along country roads via Brickendon and the Broxbourne Wood area. GR 338068. Telephone 01992 468001; web site: www.pwpark.com

The White Horse

THE HALFWAY POINT OF THIS WALK IS THE DELIGHTFUL RIVER MIMRAM, AND TEWIN BURY FARM WITH ITS HOTEL AND RESTAURANT. THE ROUTE FOLLOWS FIELD AND WOODLAND EDGES BUT IS ITSELF ALMOST ENTIRELY OUT IN THE OPEN. IT ENJOYS SOME FINE VIEWS – AT THE COST OF ONLY TWO SHORT EASY HILLS.

THE WHITE HORSE – how many visitors to this pub will have come and gone without realising that the horse is headless? It is said that a white horse lost its head hereabouts in a scuffle during the Civil War, and that at night its headless body can be seen galloping down Whitehorse Lane.

There is nothing sombre about the White Horse today. It is a truly attractive pub. The public bar is cosily furnished with traditional settles, while the adjoining restaurant, equally comfortable, leads to the patio and the garden. Children may be taken into the restaurant area.

Food is available lunchtimes and evenings, Monday to Friday; all day Saturday; and 12 noon to 4 pm on Sunday; and you pay the same whether you use the bar or the restaurant. There is a wide choice from simple fare to main meals. The evening menu is distinctly more special, ideal if you have something to celebrate. There are usually three real ales on offer: Greene King IPA, Adnams and Bass. Drinking hours are all day, every day, which here means 11 am to midnight. If Fido is with you, I am afraid you will have to leave him outside.

✆ 01438 798100.

How to get there: The pub overlooks the green. If you are coming from the A1(M) near Welwyn (not Welwyn Garden City) join the A1000 from junction 6 (Hertford direction) and go forward into Hertford Road (Digswell direction) when the A1000 turns right; then turn left into Harmer Green Lane just beyond the magnificent Digswell viaduct. Stay in this road all the way to Burnham Green – even when it changes its name to New Road and back again.
Parking: In front of the pub or alongside the green.
Length of the walk: 4½ miles. Map: OS Landranger 166 Luton, Hertford and surrounding area (GR 262166).

THE WALK

1 From the White Horse and White Horse Lane go over the road crossing on Burnham Green and into Orchard Road,

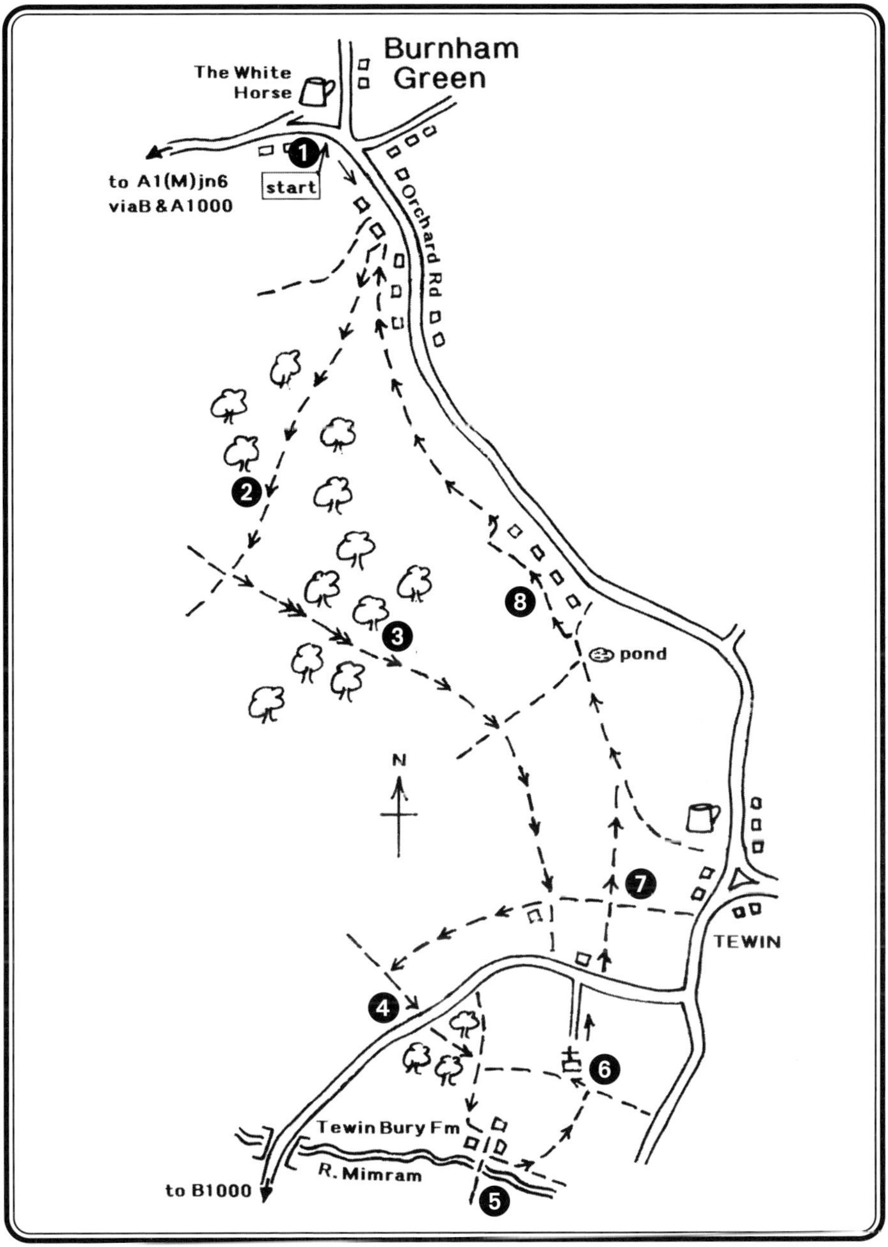
Burnham Green
The White Horse
start
to A1(M)jn6 viaB&A1000
Orchard Rd
pond
N
TEWIN
Tewin Bury Fm
R. Mimram
to B1000
1
2
3
4
5
6
7
8

passing in sight of a former hostelry, the Duck. On the right in Orchard Road you will find the old infant school, now the village hall, and a pair of houses numbered 26 and 28. Go through the gap immediately after the houses and soon cross the short sharp corner of a field (240°), not along the field's left-hand edge. As soon as you enter the next field you should turn left (170°), placing your back to a stile and its complicated waymark post.

Follow the hedge on the left and, later, a wood edge on the right. In the far distance Welwyn Garden City comes into view as you descend the hill and go through a kissing gate into the field ahead.

2 After leaving the wood edge your path keeps straight on, but now across a field (210°) and with a prominent tower block directly ahead. At the next crossing track turn left (downhill) and soon go uphill through a gap in the trees. In sight over your right shoulder as you ascend the hill is Digswell Viaduct carrying the railway that runs from Kings Cross to the North. It has 40 arches and was built using five million bricks.

3 The track breaks out into the open and runs down to a crossing (which could be mistaken for a T-junction) where you should continue straight on between the trees. At the next crossing just prior to a cottage turn right so that the cottage and its garden hedge is on your left and a field on your right. From the end of what is a very long hedge keep straight on across the fields (with that distant tower block still directly ahead) to its T-junction with another track.

4 Turn left here and follow a hedge and iron fence to a road. Cross the road to the woodland path opposite and follow this through until you meet a rough drive running beyond the far side of the wood. Turn right and go downhill in the drive to Tewin Bury Farm, now a hotel and restaurant – and

much else besides. Go left along a concrete path and soon right by the old farmhouse. This will take you to the delightful river Mimram from where the sluices of a former watermill can be seen.

5 Do not cross the bridge here but turn left and follow a track parallel to the river for 100 yards only. Branch half-left here and cross the grass, staying in the dip of the hillside and passing about 50 yards left of a small abandoned quarry. Strictly speaking you should follow the dip up as far as a fence and turn left towards St Peter's church and churchyard. Alternatively you could enjoy the freedom to roam that seems to exist here, by taking a more direct route to the church.

6 Once in the churchyard via its nearest (south-east) corner, you could pass to the east of the church. Here will you find the grave of Lady Anne Grimston who died in 1713 (the units digit on the stone is not clear). She is reported to have said, 'If indeed there is life hereafter, trees will render asunder my tomb'. See what you think!

Leave the church along its drive and turn right in the road opposite the imposing Old Rectory, then soon go through a gate signposted 'Upper Green ½' just beyond an attractive timber-framed barn. From here walk the fenced path to a gate at the far end (10°). Having passed through that gate you could divert to Tewin village if you wish. It has a green, a few nice cottages, a village shop and two pubs. Simply turn right and soon take one of the two branches into the village.

7 Back at the gate cross the very large field ahead, maintaining (almost) the same direction as before (360°). This will lead you into a long a narrow field and forward again to a lovely tree-lined sunken track (Back Lane) in which you should turn left. You will pass a pond on the right before the track

curves right alongside a sports field. When you are halfway round that curve join a narrow path through the trees and scrub on the left. On emerging, turn right and soon join a field edge.

8 The path follows the backs of well-kept gardens for a while, and after a brief foray to the right crosses open country between fields and with a hedge on the right. It passes a single large oak tree and continues forward, following overhead wires and cutting off a large field corner. After this there are more gardens to accompany you to the road at Burnham Green. Turn left in the road for the White Horse.

PLACES OF INTEREST NEARBY

Tewin Orchard is 1 mile south of Burnham Green to the north of Tewin village centre (GR 267155). Originally planted in 1933, the orchard has been restored with traditional fruit varieties. It is managed by the Herts and Middlesex Wildlife Trust, telephone number 01727 858901; Web site: www.wildlifetrust.org.uk/herts

Welwyn Roman Baths are situated *under* the A1(M) where it links to the A1000. You may have noticed the entrance sign while driving from junction 6 of the A1(M) to Burnham Green. (GR 235156). The baths are open at weekends and Bank Holidays 2 pm to 5 pm (or dusk) and at the same times from Monday to Friday during school holidays. There is a small admission charge for adults. Telephone: 01707 272511.

The Woodhall Arms

A WALK THAT FOLLOWS MORE THAN 1 MILE OF THE LOVELY RIVER BEANE. A MARVELLOUS OUTING FOR ANYONE WHO FINDS PLEASURE IN TREES AND SHRUBS AND WATERSIDE PLANTS – AND WHO HOPES ONE DAY TO SEE A KINGFISHER.

THE WOODHALL ARMS, a popular pub on the road from Hertford, has much to recommend it. In addition to the traditional bar it has two restaurant areas and a conservatory. It is now the only pub/restaurant remaining in the village.

The Woodhall Arms is open every day at the traditional hours, with food available every lunchtime and evening. The bar menu includes starters and snacks, freshly made sandwiches, hot and cold filled baguettes and pasta dishes.

From the 'Selection of old Favourites' you could choose one of the old-fashioned English dishes – lamb's liver and onions, or steak and ale pie, for example; or you might opt for the dish that sounds somewhat more special – chicken and honey roast ham in a white wine and cream sauce.

Ale fanciers will find that the choice is between three 'regulars' and two 'guests', the former being Adnams, IPA and Youngs. There is also a wide range of interesting-flavoured soft drinks. Families are welcome here, and children have their own menu. Dogs may be taken into the bar only.

✆ 01992 535123.

How to there there: The pub stands beside the A119 at Stapleford, 2½ miles north of Hertford.
Parking: In the pub's car park beside the A119. You could alternatively drive the first part of the walk and park near Stapleford church. This will also save you a small amount of road walking!
Length of the walk: 3½ miles. Map: OS Landranger 166 Luton, Hertford and surrounding area (GR 311173).

THE WALK

1 On leaving the Woodhall Arms turn left into the A119 and first left into Church Lane. After crossing the river Beane leave the road and go along the church drive. Enter the churchyard through a gate, and, passing to the right of the church, soon join the riverside path from another gate.

2 The next ½ mile is marked with numbered posts: stages along a nature trail prepared by the Herts and Middlesex Wildlife Trust. The trail leaflet hints that a kingfisher 'might catch your eye as a spectacular flash of blue'. Such a sighting would make the day complete.

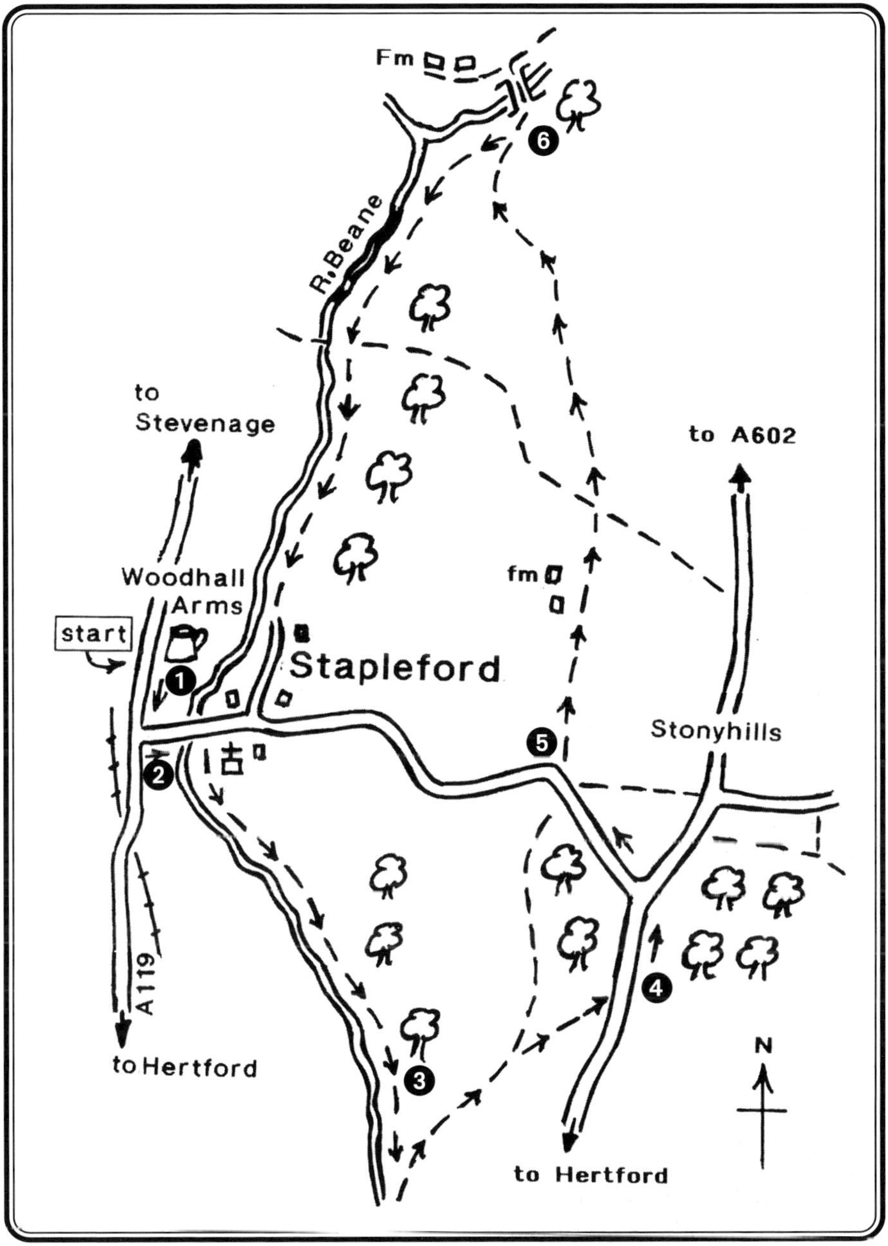
Fm
6
R. Beane
to
Stevenage
to A602
Woodhall
Arms
fm
start
1
Stapleford
5
Stonyhills
2
A119
4
N
to Hertford
3
to Hertford

3 The riverside path follows the length of Foxley's Wood before finally emerging into the open, where it turns half-left and runs briefly uphill to meet a tarmac drive. Turn left in the drive – so that the wood is on your left – and stay with it as it leaves the wood edge and runs uphill between fields. When you are midway between one wood and the next (at a left curve in the drive) leave the drive and cross a field half-right (70°) uphill towards what at first appears to be the right-hand extremity of the second wood.

4 When you reach the road from the furthest corner of the field go left and follow the road straight on. Branch left into a narrow lane after 150 yards where the left-hand wood terminates; and when the lane turns sharp left go forward into a track to Southend Farm.

5 You may now lay this book to one side while you walk the wide 1 mile track to its meeting with two short (very short) tributaries of the river Beane. Towards the end of this mile you will have passed into the walled estate of Woodhall Park, the house itself having come into view earlier. Although you will need to go into the meadow on the left just prior to the first bridge (over the first tributary) you may wish to continue in the track a little further for the view, and then come back.

6 Cross the meadow to a kissing-gate (240° and almost doubling back on your previous direction) and continue forward across the grass to the bank of the river Beane. You now have the unparalleled delight of resuming your walk alongside this lovely river; but before getting into the swing of it you will need to make your exit from Woodhall Park Estate by climbing over a brick wall. Fortunately a ladder-stile is provided! After ⅔ mile the path runs into a residential cul-de-sac at Stapleford. Turn right at the far end of this and, for the Woodhall Arms, right at the A119.

The Chequers Inn

IF THE NAME 'WARESIDE' SUGGESTS BEAUTY OR DELIGHT, THIS WALK WILL NOT BE A DISAPPOINTMENT, ESPECIALLY IN TERMS OF THE VALLEY WHICH WARESIDE OVERLOOKS. THIS VALLEY IS WHERE THE MEANDERING RIVER ASH FLOWS, A RIVER THAT ACCOMPANIES MORE THAN HALF OF THE WALK.

THE CHEQUERS has enjoyed the status of Pub of the Year, bestowed by a local branch of the Campaign for Real Ale, so it follows that the choice and quality of the beer from this delightful freehouse is beyond dispute. Equally, there can be no argument about the food or the comfortable old world atmosphere in which it can be enjoyed. And the total absence of fruit machines and juke boxes helps this along.

The choice of ales is changed from time to time, and amounts to about six different brews. The wide-ranging regular food menu includes steak, fish, home-made pies, 'Chequers Popular Specials', vegetarian dishes, salads and sandwiches (closed and open). It concludes with home-made sweets and puddings, cheese-board and liqueur coffees. All this every lunchtime and evening. Drinking hours are traditional from Monday to Friday, all day on Saturday and Sunday.

Parents with children are asked to eat in the restaurant area, since this is away from the bar. Children cannot be taken into the garden because there isn't one – just a few benches at the front near the road, and not the safest place for youngsters. Dogs may be taken into the bar if well behaved and kept on a lead.

You could prepare for another walk by staying overnight at the Chequers and, if your timing is right, greet the new day with one of their occasional Scottish breakfasts.

✆ 01920 467010.

How to get there: The Chequers is easily found: on the B1004 at Wareside 2 miles east of Ware.
Parking: If the pub's small car park is full, you could park by the triangular green a short distance into the walk.
Length of the walk: 3¾ miles. Map: OS Landranger 166 Luton, Hertford and surrounding area (GR 396156).

THE WALK

1 On leaving the Chequers go right along the B1004 and soon right into a lane signposted to Babbs Green. After a few yards you will need to choose either a narrow path immediately to the right of Bourne Cottage or to stay in the lane. The path is for the sure footed and may be overgrown with nettles, but to use it will help to keep it

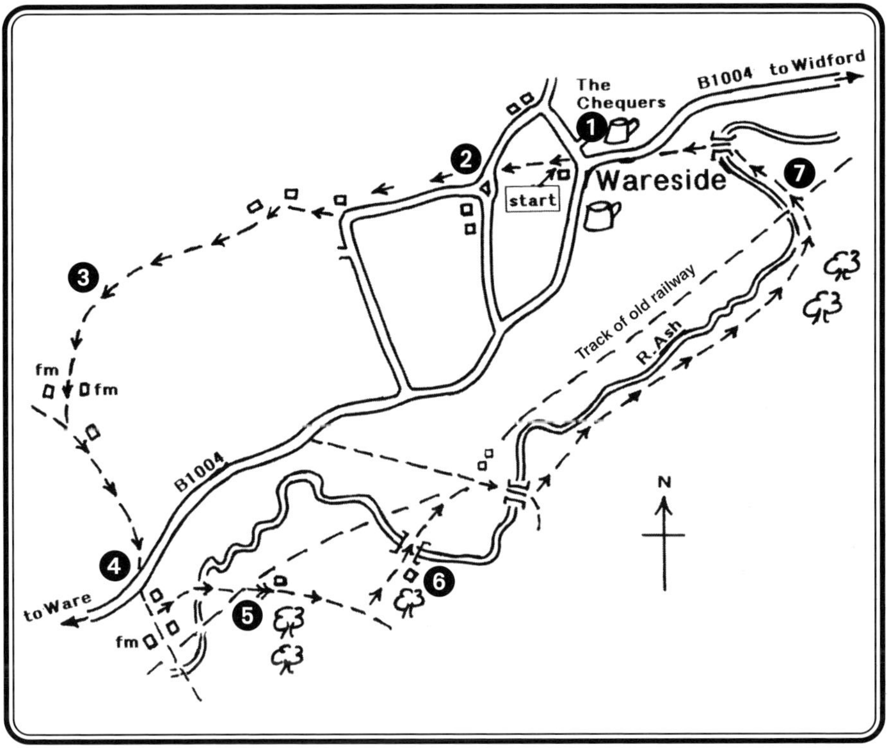

open. If you choose the lane follow it up to a T-junction by Wesley Cottage and turn left. The footpath and the lane join forces near a small triangular green adjacent to a primary school.

2 From the green go along the lane to the right of the playground and, at the junction ahead (by a pair of half-boarded houses), continue forward in a rough drive. Go left with the drive by another house (and its pond) and forward into a narrow path beyond the next, the third, house. The path runs between hedges and fields and enjoys good views, especially when the leaves have fallen.

3 In due course the path starts to descend, and is joined by another coming in from the right. It emerges into the open, passes a farm on the left and another on the right, and in the process evolves into a farm track. Ignore a track leaving from the right beyond the second farm and continue forward in the main track all the way to the B1004.

4 Cross the B1004 to the farm drive opposite and soon turn left along the grass immediately after Waters Place Farmhouse. The grass will soon lead you to a stile and into a field where you should make your way to a footbridge over the river. Having crossed the river continue in the same direction in the next field, aiming at a house on the far slope. Before reaching that house you will cross the trackbed of the former Ware, Hadham and Buntingford Railway, which was closed in 1964 after 101 years of service.

5 From the trackbed continue in the same direction, passing to the right of the house and to the left of a wood, along a track that progressively steepens. When after 150 yards you reach the near corner of another wood, leave the present track by joining another running downhill on the left (50°). The wood will then be on your right as you descend the hill, and you will pass a cottage when you arrive at the bottom. Leave the track where it soon curves left beyond the cottage and keep forward to a footbridge over the river (your second crossing and two more to go).

6 Keep straight on from the bridge along a track crossing a field then go right into another track running parallel with the disused railway. When you soon meet yet another track (crossing a railway bridge from the left) go right with it and downhill back to the river. Cross the river and turn left immediately through a gate, then walk the long narrow meadow in sight of a tennis court on the left and guided by two magnificent trees, a horse chestnut and a beech. A metal

gate at the end of the meadow leads into another meadow of similar width, and a gate at the end of this leads into a third, with the river keeping company all the while. Keep to the lowest level of the third meadow (which is overlooked by a wood uphill on the right) and aim for a railway bridge ahead.

7 After crossing the railway trackbed (immediately to the right of the bridge) and entering the field opposite, walk the river bank as far as a footbridge on the left. Once over the bridge follow the left edge of a field and its accompanying stream (a tributary of the river Ash) back to Wareside and the Chequers.

PLACE OF INTEREST NEARBY

Scott's Grotto in Ware consists of intriguing passages and chambers dug into the hillside and decorated with flints, shells and pebbles. It is open from April to the end of September every Saturday and Bank Holiday Monday from 2 pm to 4.30 pm. It is situated in Scotts Road (which is off Hertford Road) between houses numbered 28 and 34. (GR 357138). A donation is suggested. Telephone 01920 464131; web site: www.scotts-grotto.org

The Prince of Wales

THIS MUST BE ONE OF THE MOST INTERESTING AND ENJOYABLE WALKS IN THE COUNTY. AFTER 1 MILE OF FIELD EDGES IT ENTERS PERRY GREEN, A VILLAGE ASSOCIATED WITH THE SCULPTOR HENRY MOORE. IT FORDS THE RIVER ASH (THERE IS A FOOTBRIDGE) AND FOLLOWS PART OF MUCH HADHAM'S FABULOUS HIGH STREET, LOOPING BACK ACROSS DELIGHTFUL RIVER MEADOWS BEFORE RETURNING TO GREEN TYE.

THE PRINCE OF WALES, out of the four pubs that lie on or close to the walk, has something very special to offer: it owns and runs its very own microbrewery. It is here that labels such as Union Jack, Bateman Hopbine, Mad Morris and Ditch Diver (to name but a few) bring delight to the real ale enthusiast.

On the food front, dishes such as steak and kidney pie, Green Tye curry, home-made game stew and ploughman's represent the pub's no-nonsense fare which can be enjoyed daily from 12 noon to 2 pm.

The pub is open from 12 noon to 3 pm and 5.30 pm to midnight on Monday to Friday, 12 noon to 1 am on Saturday (yes 1 am!), 11.15 am to 11 pm on Sunday.

Families are welcome, and children's meals are available. Dogs are also welcome – well behaved ones of course! In summer the large garden to the side of the pub can be enjoyed by all.

✆ 01279 842517.

A more extensive range of meals is available at the Hoops Inn, Perry Green, one mile into the walk (✆ 01279 843568) and at the Old Crown, Hadham Cross, (✆ 01279 842753).

How to get there: Green Tye is best approached from the B1004 3 miles south-west of Bishops Stortford. It is signposted from the B1004 opposite the entrance to Great Hadham Golf Club. The pub is a short distance beyond the green.
Parking: In the pub's car park or alongside the green.
Length of the walk: 5 miles. Map: OS Landranger 167 Chelmsford, Harlow and surrounding area (GR 443184).

THE WALK

1 On leaving the pub turn sharp right immediately into the drive signposted (from the roadside opposite) as a public byway. When this runs into a private entrance just beyond thatched Green Tye Cottage, continue forward in a footpath between hedges. At the T-junction ahead turn right and follow a ditch and the right-hand edge of a field, while ignoring a path crossing the field half-left. When confronted

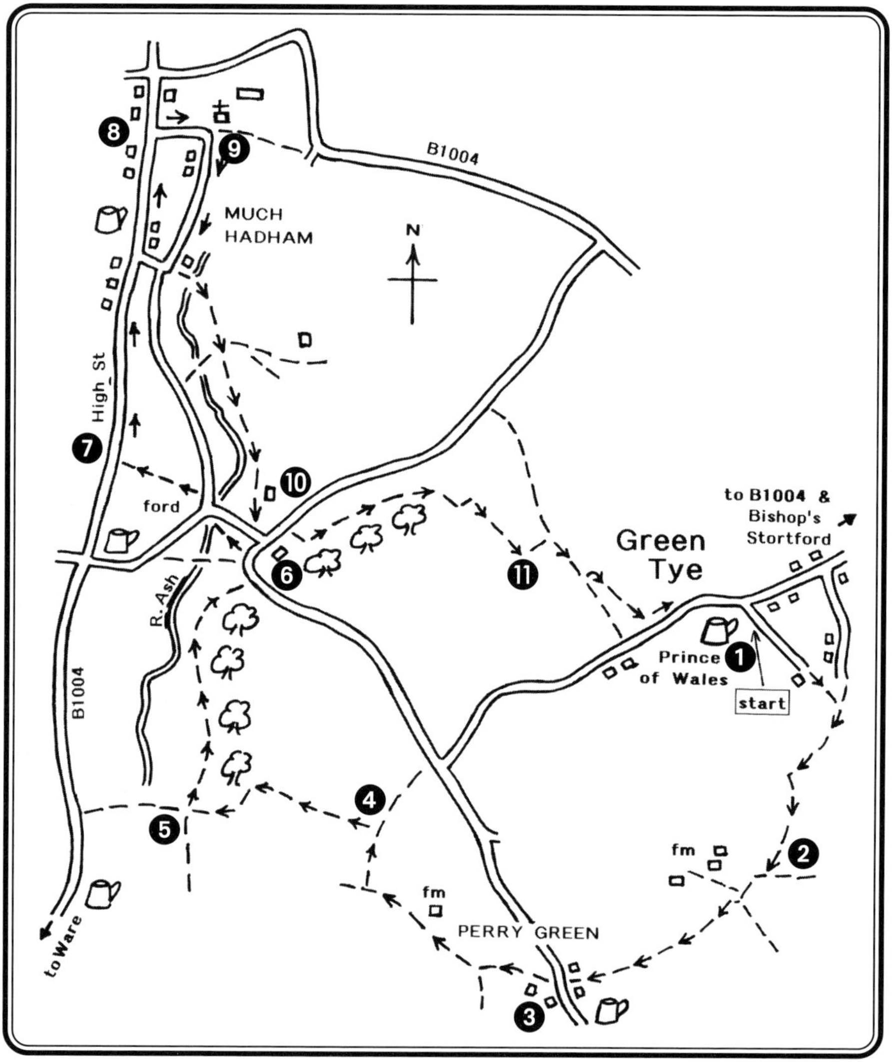

by a hedge and another ditch at the first corner of the field, turn left and follow the meandering hedge and ditch (on your right), generally heading in the direction of farm buildings.

2 When close to the farm your path turns right and is joined by another coming in from the left. When it soon goes off to the left (now as a track across the fields) turn right around the second of two ponds and into a field corner (not into the farm drive). Then follow a ditch and hedge on the right all the way along the field (a very long field) to a gap in its far right-hand corner. The gap will place you on Perry Green's green and a left turn in the road (if you wish) will place you in front of another very nice pub, the Hoops Inn.

3 From the green, cross over to a drive (signposted as a footpath) leading to Danetree House and the grounds of the Henry Moore Foundation. Noting examples of Henry Moore's work on all sides, stay with the drive (initially straight on) until it turns left; then go forward across the grass to a stile and into a field. Turn slightly right from the stile (320°) and follow the field edge uphill (there's a stile en-route), passing to the left of a farm and continuing forward across the fields. Do not rush on, but turn right into a path about 50 yards *before* a stile and metal gate and the extremity of an infilled gravel working – which you would hardly recognise as such. The path runs between fields divided by a very few trees (10°).

4 After 120 yards turn left at a path junction (by a tall oak tree) into a wide grassy track leading to a distant wood. On arrival at the wood turn left and follow its edge (wood right, field left) firstly straight on, then round to the right. Leaving the wood behind drop steeply downhill, following overhead wires to a stile (or gap) at the bottom.

5 Turn right at a crossing path soon after the stile (i.e. do not go ahead over a footbridge) and follow a path which soon runs just inside the wood (the same wood as previously, but lower down). If you stay on the level and take guidance from the occasional waymark, you will in due

course (⅓ mile) arrive at a road. In attempting to avoid mud, some walkers have followed a parallel route deeper in the wood.

6 Go left in the road, and when it soon turns right keep forward through a pedestrian gate and into a meadow. Maintaining the same direction, cross the meadow to its far right-hand corner (near two 30 mph signs) and go over the stile there. Cross the ford and join a path running uphill opposite. This will eventually place you in Much Hadham's High Street, where you should turn right.

7 Making your way along the High Street you could hardly fail to notice Forge Cottage (with its museum, Victorian kitchen garden and working blacksmith) and Hopley's Garden and Nursery opposite The Hall. Do have a look at the garden; not only is it very attractive, but entry is free.

8 When you are almost out of the village take the turning down to St Andrew's church; then tarry in this lovely place. The north side of the churchyard is a good point from which to see the impressive five-gabled palace, for many years the country retreat of the Bishops of London. And inside the church is what must surely be the finest and most varied collection of kneelers anywhere!

9 Go right with the road by the church and follow it through until it turns right again; then at a gate in the corner turn left alongside the garden of Two Bridges. A concrete footbridge will soon place you in a meadow which you should cross more or less straight on (160°). Pass through a kissing-gate in the far left-hand corner and cross a rough drive to another kissing-gate (not to the gate half-left).

The path through the next meadow is fairly obvious and heads in the direction of farm buildings – while the river flows its twisting course over to the right. Where the meadow is divided by a kissing-gate and fence, you should go half-right towards the far left-hand corner, where there's a kissing gate and a road (190°).

10 From whatever point you join the road turn left in it and left again at a T-junction; then leave the road just beyond a garden and cross a footbridge and stile leading into a field. Go left along the field to a stile at the far end and forward under the trees. The path turns right just before the trees give way to a field. Go uphill with the path to an old oak tree and straight on along the (perhaps faint) boundary between the fields (140°). If you aim at a house-top on the horizon and slightly left of a wooden electricity pole, you can't go far wrong.

11 When you are confronted by another field higher up (there is no dividing hedge or fence) a few yards before overhead wires, turn left along a grassy path (60°) and, passing under the wires, soon make contact with a track at a T-junction. Turn right in the track and follow this and its accompanying ditch across the fields until you come close to trees on the left.

The remaining stretch of the walk – to the road at Green Tye – runs through those trees parallel to the track and is indicated by a waymark post. Since the entrance to the path may not be obvious (just a hole in the trees 15 yards to the left of the track) you could be forgiven for staying in the open as far as the road at Green Tye. Once at the road, turn left and follow this back to the Prince of Wales.

The Bull Inn

NOT ONLY DOES THIS WALK START AND FINISH AT A MOST DELIGHTFUL VILLAGE, BUT IT ALSO TRAVERSES SOME FINE HERTFORDSHIRE COUNTRYSIDE, WITH GOOD VIEWS OF THE NEIGHBOURING HILLS. IT PASSES THROUGH ST PAUL'S WALDEN WHERE THE CHURCH HAS CLOSE ASSOCIATIONS WITH THE LATE QUEEN MOTHER. SHE WAS BAPTISED HERE ON 23RD SEPTEMBER 1900.

THE BULL INN dating back to at least 1675, and always thought of as Whitwell's leading inn, today retains much of its old world atmosphere. The public bar and the saloon bar each have real log fires; so this is the perfect venue at which to end a winter walk. In summer the garden is perhaps the best place to be, with its view of the lovely Mimram valley.

Meals are served daily, but at lunch times only (12 noon to 2.30 pm). The wide-ranging menu includes an excellent variety of sandwiches, soups, and ploughmans, and a choice of around twelve main meals. You could walk on a Wednesday and take advantage of a good value, two-course lunch that is offered weekly on that day. The sweets menu is difficult to ignore, with its delicious choices. On Sunday the lunchtime menu is limited to soup, sandwiches, a traditional roast and sweets. Children are very welcome; they can choose a meal from the special Junior Menu. The separate dining room is ideally suited for family eating.

There is usually a choice of around three real ales, including a 'guest'. The inn is open all day, every day, winter and summer. Well-behaved dogs are welcome in the bars or in the garden.

✆ 01438 871254.

How to get there: Whitwell is on the B651 halfway between Hitchin and Harpenden. To connect with the B651 take the B656 from Hitchen or the B652 from Harpenden, via Kimpton.
Parking: In the pub's own car park or along the roadside nearby.
Length of the walk: 4¼ miles. Map: OS Landranger 166 Luton, Hertford and surrounding area (GR 184212).

THE WALK

1 After turning left out of the Bull and walking along Whitwell's lovely old High Street, it is interesting to recall a commentary written in 1908 and to know that some things change for the better:

Its situation along the valley of the river is very pretty, but the village itself is unpleasing, being a long row of houses which are for the most part, poor.

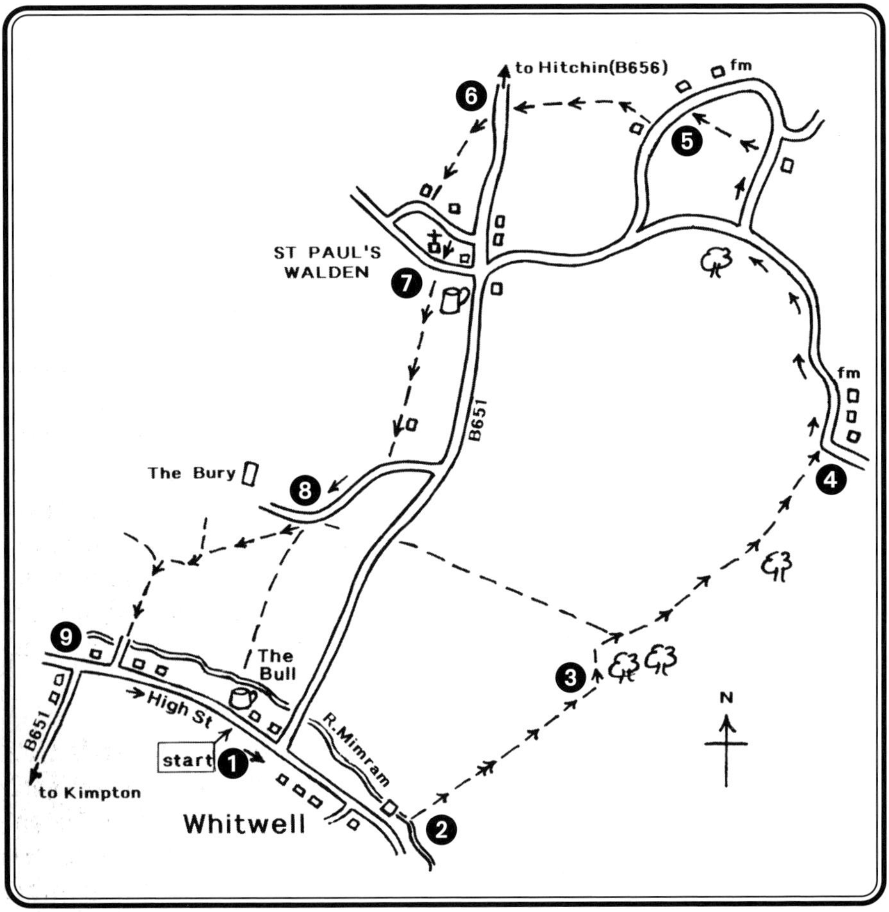

2 From a T-junction by the war memorial keep straight on (for Codicote), and after ¼ mile turn left into a public byway immediately beyond Rose Farm. This track takes you over the river Mimram then slightly left (do not go into the right-hand field here) and uphill. As you tackle the ¼ mile steady climb it would be a serious omission not to glance back at the view of Whitwell and the Mimram valley.

3 After the track levels out it takes a left-hand turn (not to be confused with a branch leaving from the left earlier), and within 100 yards reverts to its previous direction. After a further 50 yards there is an easily missed view (over your left shoulder) of The Bury at the far end of a long avenue of lime trees. The Bury is where the late Queen Elizabeth the Queen Mother spent part of her childhood and where members of her family (the Bowes Lyons) still live. We will pass close to the house later in the walk.

4 In less than ½ mile the track joins a lane at a bend. Keep forward here, soon passing East Hall Farm with its pond, ducks and hens. Stay in the lane when it soon curves left (i.e. ignore the farm road going straight on) and continue for ⅓ mile to a road junction where there is another pond. Turn right here (for Shilley Green and Langley) and continue for a further ¼ mile to another junction. From this junction go into a field on the left, as directed by a footpath signpost. Cross the field (300°) to a stile in the far left-hand corner, to the left of an attractive two-storey cottage.

5 Turn left in the lane here and go along this for 15 yards to a kissing-gate on the right. Cross a field half-left to another gate then follow the next field's left-hand edge (270°). When the hedge turns left (by a cattle trough) keep forward across the field (280°) to a stile by the B651. The impressive entrance gates in view half-right as you crossed that field are those of Stagenhoe Park, once the residence of the composer Sir Arthur Sullivan, now a Sue Ryder Home for the physically handicapped.

6 Cross the B651 (very quiet for a B road) to a path opposite and follow this forward (240°) across a field for 40 yards to an electricity pole, then go half-left (200°), aiming for the (largely hidden) church at St Paul's Walden. Three tall trees followed by a hedge accompany the path to a field corner.

Keep straight on from this corner between timber fences and in a path that passes a modern house Old Meadow, after which turn left in a lane and right to the church.

Inside the church on the north wall you will find a plaque commemorating the birth 'in this parish' and the baptism 'in this church' of the late Queen Elizabeth the Queen Mother in 1900. In the tower a 700 year old stained glass window depicts the Virgin and Child, but you will need to peep behind the tower curtain to see the window at its best – against the daylight.

Having passed through the churchyard to the south gate a short diversion may now be made (depending on the state of thirst) to the Strathmore Arms by turning left in the lane.

7 From the south gate, and with your back to the church, cross the lane to a track opposite (signposted as a footpath) and follow this downhill for ⅓ mile to where it joins a tarmac drive. Just prior to the drive you will have passed Garden House on your left and a lake almost out of sight on the right. Go right and uphill in the drive and cross that magnificent lime avenue – with its view of The Bury – noted earlier in the walk.

8 Ignore a kissing-gate on the left before the drive starts to curve right (on its way to The Bury) and go through another gate on the left at the completion of the curve, soon after a track comes in from the left, rear.

Now take care! From that second kissing-gate you will need to cross a pasture diagonally corner to corner (240°), aiming for the far end of a line of tall trees, where you may recognise a group of Scots pines. Alternatively aim slightly right of a distant water tower. Turn left into a wide path from that far corner and soon (100 yards) go left and downhill in a sunken track to Whitwell, where another left turn will see you back at the Bull.

ONE OF THE MANY FINE BUILDINGS TO BE SEEN IN WHITWELL.

9 Nine Wells Watercress Farm at the western end of the village makes an interesting diversion with which to end the day. It has been in the same family for at least 160 years and supplies watercress to Hertfordshire towns and to a London wholesale market – also to passers-by like yourself!

PLACE OF INTEREST NEARBY

The Waterhall Open Farm in Whitwell is of interest to adults and children alike. Its tea room would be a pleasant place to end your day! The farm is open at weekends and over school holidays. The entrance is located a short distance from the war memorial along the B651. Telephone: 01438 871256.

15 Benington

The Bell

A walk with two long uninterrupted valley paths, level but enjoying magnificent views – ideal if you are of a mind to step it out and cannot wait to get back to this lovely village! Or it could be that you hope to visit the Benington Lordship Gardens before returning home. (See Place of Interest Nearby)

THE BELL occupies an eminently desirable situation in one of the county's most attractive villages. Well-kept cottages, village pond, church and churchyard face each other across the green, an idyllic scene little disturbed by passing traffic.

The pub complements and enhances the village with its presence, not least through its welcome and comfort, its good food and its good drink. Whether you prefer simple pub fare or a hot main meal, you can be assured of good quality food in substantial proportions. Although four real ales are offered (IPA, Abbot Ale and two guests which change monthly) this is overshadowed by another much wider choice – 28 malt whiskies.

Children over seven can be taken into the dining-room if having meals, but they would be just as happy in the garden, where they could watch Dad play pétanque. Dogs are allowed in the garden only.

✆ 01438 869270.

How to get there: From the A1(M) near Stevenage, join the A602 from junction 7 (Stevenage direction, then Hertford direction from the first roundabout) and turn left after 2 miles into Aston Lane at Bragbury End opposite a garden centre. Follow the road signs to Aston (not Aston End) and turn sharp right out of Aston for Benington.
Parking: In the pub's car park or along the roadside if the car park is full. Please do not use the pub's car park unless you are a customer; and please get the landlord's permission if you wish to leave your car there while on the walk.
Length of the walk: 4½ miles. Map: OS Landranger 166 Luton, Hertford and surrounding area (GR 301235).

THE WALK

1 From the road junction on the green (adjacent to the village pond) go downhill in the Aston direction, passing the parish church on your right.

2 Ignore the first track on the left (the one going forward and uphill near a Benington road sign) and continue to the

second. This is 50 yards beyond a kissing gate on the left. Follow this track (a byway) between hedges and under electricity wires to a fenced pumping station. At a T-junction in the track here turn left and follow another set of wires along the dip of the fields, with a ditch on the left.

3 After ⅓ mile the track turns left and runs uphill. Keep straight on here, along a footpath and still following the ditch and the wires. When you arrive at a hedge corner after 200 yards (adjacent to an electricity pole), turn right and go uphill along the field edge (180°) for half its length to a gap at the far end of the hedge. Go through the gap into the sharp end of a field and go up towards a cottage, where a metal gate will lead you into a lane. Follow this lane to the road at Burn's Green by the Lordship Arms.

4 Cross to Hebing End opposite (a no through road) and go with it to its end. You cannot go wrong: there is a pond at the beginning of the road and a pond at the end. When the tarmac terminates just beyond the second pond, turn right into a bridleway running between a field left and a garden right. After 60 yards the track turns left and takes a level route along a left-hand field edge (about 60°). It drops downhill along the next field edge (there is woodland in view beyond the right-hand field edge) to a gap near the bottom of the valley.

5 Go through the gap to another field and forward to a footbridge *but not over it*. Turn left here so that a ditch is on your right and enjoy this marvellous 1 mile valley walk. It is interrupted twice only: by a private track leaving from the left after ⅓ mile and by an oblique crossing track after a further ⅓ mile. The latter is just beyond a tree-planted triangle and comes down from Benington Park. Continue straight on, briefly under the trees and resuming your previous direction along the dip of the fields.

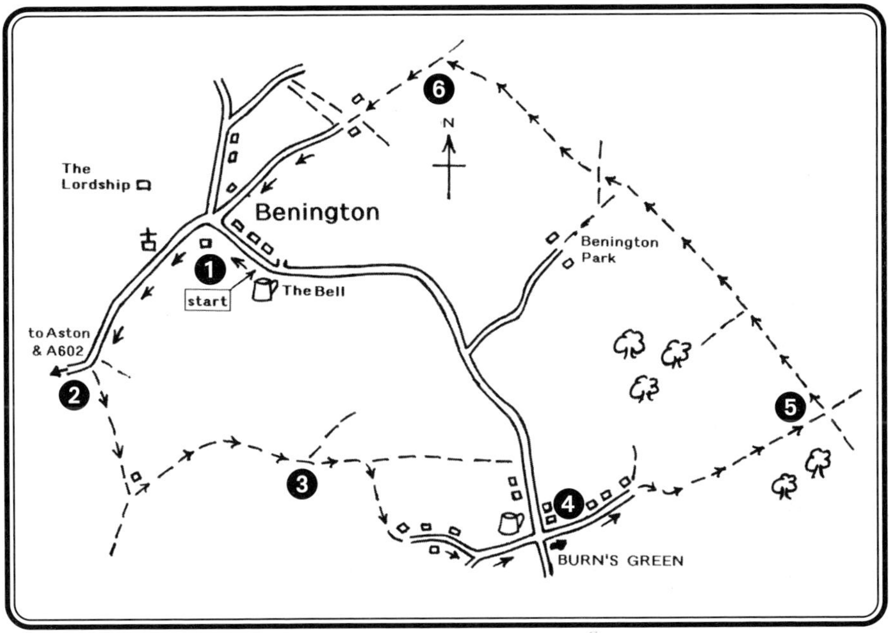

6 Go through a hedge gap at the far end into another field and turn left immediately, then join a track going uphill under trees. Stay with this track as it eventually evolves into tarmacked Duck Lane, a name which becomes meaningful when you arrive at the pond in Benington.

PLACE OF INTEREST NEARBY

Benington Lordship Gardens are a delight at any time of the year, but especially so during high summer days when the herbaceous borders are at their best. Telephone: 08701 261709; www.beningtonlordship.co.uk

16 Great Offley

The Green Man

If you have any reservations about the beauty and variety of Hertfordshire's countryside, this walk should put them to rest. It commences with a lovely ½ mile of quiet lane (a no through road) with some of the county's finest views. After passing Little Offley (a Tudor manor house) it returns to Great Offley through woods and across fields that seem to be on top of the world.

THE GREEN MAN has a slogan 'open 8 days a week' – it is not very far from the truth. If you arrive here any time between 11.30 am and 10 pm Monday to Saturday you can enjoy a meal. On Sunday the times are 11.30 am to 9.30 pm. The manager of this Chef and Brewer pub is proud of his 'good value food', much of which is prepared on the premises. 'You will not find plastic food here!' he says. The wide range of meals – at prices to suit most pockets – can be enjoyed in the bar area or in the light and airy conservatory. You could alternatively eat in the garden, where there is a marvellous view across country. If you wish to make your visit more of an occasion in itself you could dine in the restaurant.

The pub is open for drinking virtually all day every day from 11 am to 11 pm. Real ales number three or four, with different brews being offered from time to time.

Children are made very welcome, the conservatory or the garden being ideal for them. There is an attractive and safe play area at the front of the pub. Dogs are also welcome, but in the front garden only, and assuming they are on their best behaviour.

✆ 01462 768256.

How to get there: Great Offley is well signposted from the A505 halfway between Luton and Hitchin. Bus 102 from Hitchin runs hourly Monday to Saturday, bus 101 hourly Sunday. There is a good rail service daily from London (Kings Cross) to Hitchin. You will find the pub close to the main village crossing.
Parking: In the pub's car park or along the roadside, especially near the church in High Street.
Length of the walk: 4 miles. Map: OS Landranger 166 Luton, Hertford and surrounding area (GR 142271).

THE WALK

1 From the Green Man go over the crossing into School Lane, not failing to notice the timber-framed dovecote along the farm drive on the left, or the farmhouse. Follow the lane

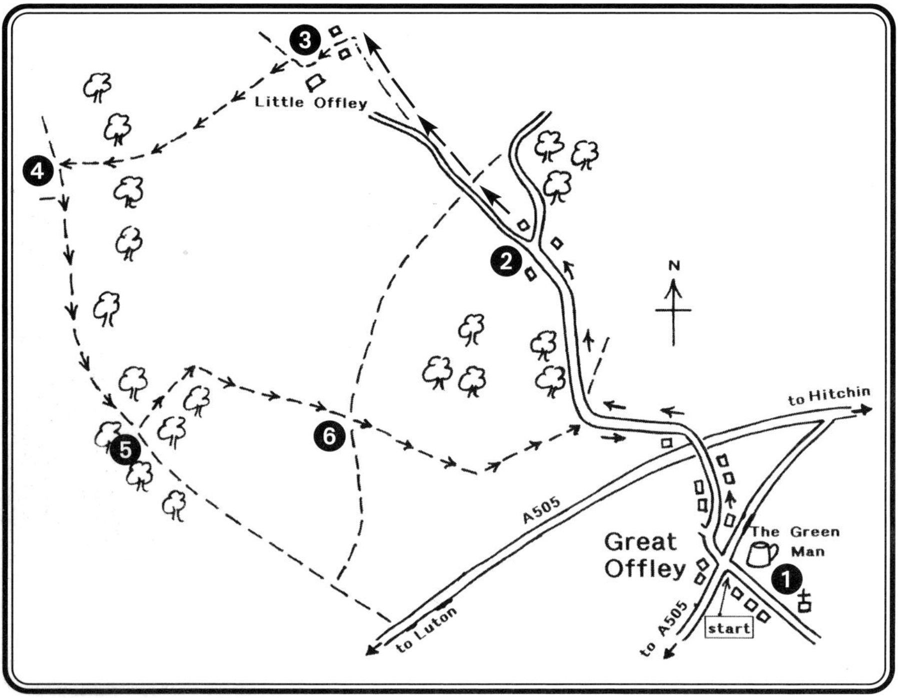

over the bypass and stay with it for ½ mile until it branches two ways.

2 Take the left-hand option (straight on for Little Offley) and follow this drive, eventually over a crossing, to where it bears slightly to the left. Leave the drive at this point and walk the field edge on the right, with a line of trees on your left. On leaving the field edge from the far left-hand corner, turn left between a stable block and a barn.

3 Progressing along a field edge, you will soon pass the Tudor manor house. Follow the field edge as it curves right, and when it comes out of the curve resume your previous direction by joining a track on the left along a left-hand field

edge (240°). If there is a tall pylon emerging from the trees directly ahead (distantly), then chances are you are on the right course.

Follow the hedge all the way to the field's far left-hand corner. Once there enter a wood and keep straight on to the far side. When you emerge from the trees cross a field to the hedge opposite – and feel yourself on top of the world.

OFFLEY'S ATTRACTIVE VILLAGE SIGN.

4 Turn left here (south) and follow the right-hand field edge, soon under electricity wires and straight on. The wood through which you have just walked will be well over to your left and a panoramic view (weather permitting) to your right. The space between you and the trees gradually diminishes as the path progresses, and you will find yourself beside a short gap between one woodland and the next.

5 Continue forward 30 yards from the gap to a path on the left running into what is a spur of this second woodland; and then start counting! After 250 man-sized paces (200 yards) along this clear path through the wood another path leaves from the left (50°). This path may not be waymarked, but you can identify it by its shortness (100 yards) and the fact that you can see the light of day at its far end.

Having gone along that path you will emerge into a field corner. Continue forward along the field edge, with trees on your immediate right, and then turn right at the following wood corner and follow the trees along for 35 yards only. From this point launch slightly left across a field along its dip (110°) to a waymark post at a hedge corner. Keep forward, with the hedge left and fields left and right; then over a crossing by a three-way electricity pylon.

6 As you follow the overhead wires straight on uphill along the next field edge, the sight and sound of the A505 will become apparent. Soon after this, and on level ground, the field edge curves left and the path (now a track) goes with it, passing between hedges (60°) and eventually meeting a road. If the track at one point is more suitable for ducks than walkers, you could take avoiding action by advancing through the trees on the left. On arrival at the road turn right and make your way back to the Green Man.

PLACE OF INTEREST NEARBY

The Hitchin Museum and Art Gallery at Paynes in nearby Hitchin contains many fascinating exhibits, including an old chemist's shop and a medicinal plant garden. It is open from 10 am to 5 pm on Monday to Saturday, with the exception of Wednesday and Bank Holidays. Admission is free. Telephone: 01462 434476; web site www.north-herts.gov.uk

The Motte and Bailey

THE FOUR SUPERLATIVES THAT PASSED THROUGH MY MIND WHEN I FIRST WALKED THIS ROUTE WERE: 'GREAT FIELDS, GREAT WOODS, GREAT VIEWS, GREAT WALK.' CHOOSE A FINE DAY AND YOU COULD WELL EXPERIENCE THE SAME EMOTIONS – ASSUMING THAT YOU ARE HAPPY WITH THE LONG STEADY ASCENT THAT MARKS THE FIRST HALF OF THE WALK.

THE MOTTE AND BAILEY, with its idyllic location overlooking Pirton's Great Green and its closeness to some magnificent open country, has 'everything going for it'. The pub's name reflects the one-time existence of a Norman castle near the church. We will see its huge mound – the motte – as we approach the end of the walk.

Inside, the Motte and Bailey (the pub!) is very pleasantly furnished – an ideal setting for that end-of-walk meal. This could be one of the home-made pies, the curry or the lasagne, followed by a choice from that list of delicious-sounding sweets (how could you resist that chocolate fudge cake)! On Sunday you can enjoy a roast lunch or one of its alternatives – scampi or gammon perhaps. All this at lunchtimes and evenings from Monday to Saturday, Sunday 12 noon to 5pm. If you are 'of a certain age', you can, from Monday to Thursday, avail yourself of an 'OAP meal'!

Real ales are John Smith's, IPA, and Spitfire, with Adnams as a guest. The pub is open all day, every day, from 12 noon.

Families are very welcome here, and children can choose from their own menu. Dogs are also welcome inside.

✆ 01462 712641.

How to get there: The pub is located in Great Green, not far from Pirton's parish church. If approaching from Hitchin, which is 2½ miles south-east of Pirton, join the B655 (from the A505, Luton direction) and branch right into an unclassified road after 1 mile.
Parking: In the pub's car park or along the roadside nearby.
Length of the walk: 4¼ miles. Map: OS Landranger 166 Luton, Hertford and surrounding area (GR 145315).

THE WALK

1 Turn left out of the pub and, with the green on your right, stay on the road to its junction with Hitchin Road/Priors Hill. When you cross this to the track opposite (beside a transformer and signposted 'Public Bridleway') you are at the start of a marvellous uninterrupted ascent (ignore all branches) taking you to a height of 400 feet in 1 mile. Included in the view as you climb is the church at Shillington prominently sited on a mound and a prehistoric burial mound in sight after you pass a wood on the right.

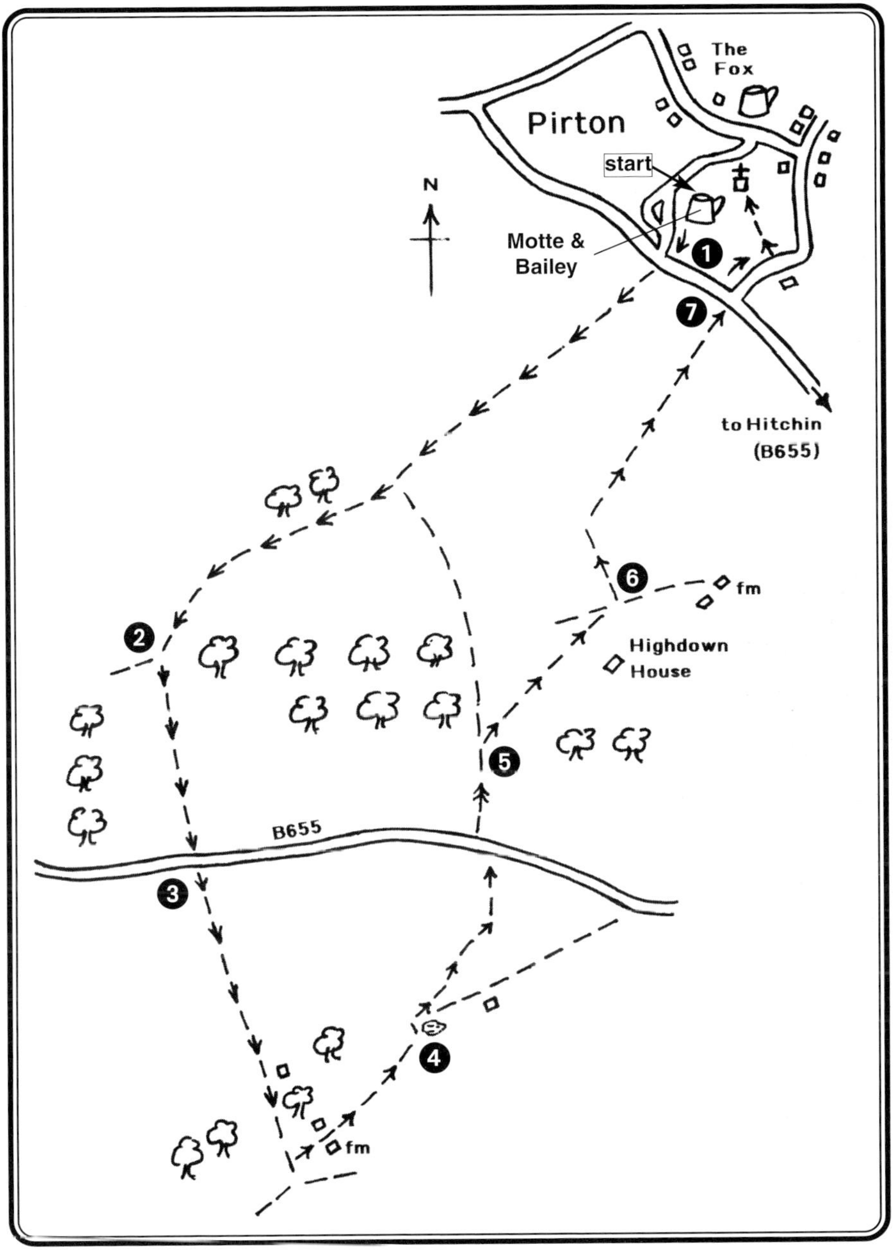
The Fox
Pirton
start
N
Motte & Bailey
1
7
to Hitchin (B655)
2
6
fm
Highdown House
5
B655
3
4
fm

2 The termination of that 1 mile climb coincides with the far end of a stretch of woodland on the left. Here a waymark post marks the division of the route into two, and if you continue forward a few more yards you have a prospect of a very fine view westward across Hexton and the Burton Hills in Bedfordshire. Back at the waymark post you should take the left-hand branch in the track and follow a hedge and overhead wires to the B655 road.

3 Cross the road to a wide track signposted to New Wellbury Farm. Deacon Hill makes its appearance ½ mile westward as you ascend the gently sloping track and approach Woodland Cottage. Beyond the cottage a stretch of woodland hides farm buildings and leads you forward towards a T-junction. Just before the junction a waymark arrow on the left directs you through the trees and alongside an iron fence to a kissing-gate. Go forward between farm buildings (New Wellbury Farm), then between fields and uphill in a wide grassy track (40°), passing a water-filled pit on the right at the top.

4 The track soon turns left then right, skirting a pond on the right and meeting a kissing-gate adjacent to an electricity pole. A little concentration is now required. Do not be tempted into the track running forward from the stile along the right-hand field edge, but cross the field itself about quarter-left with respect to the track (30°). You will pass about 40 yards left of a double pole electricity pylon, with a farmhouse downhill beyond that.

Following the waymarks, you will eventually pass to the left of an overgrown pit before being led downhill to a road. Cross the road to a footpath opposite and turn right after 40 yards into a field. Descend the dip of the field and climb the steep slope opposite, following the left-hand hedge to a kissing-gate at the top and into another field.

5 Your utmost concentration is required yet again! Cross the field roughly halfway between the left-hand wood and the right-hand house (40°). This direction is a little right of Pirton church, now coming into view ahead, and will take you within 150 yards of the house. Much of this lovely stone-built house (High Down) dates back to the late 1500s or thereabouts. Notice the ornate weather vane; it may help you in getting the correct bearing across this field.

6 As you pass the house go downhill to a kissing-gate where four fields join (not the 'private' stile), then turn left immediately in the field ahead, with a hedge now on your left (340°). The rest is easy. Follow the hedge (the church is half-right now) to its far corner by an electricity pole which has wires branching three ways. Turn right here and follow the wires and the left-hand hedge down to Hitchin Road.

7 Join Walnut Tree Road opposite and go through a gate on the left after a few yards or through another gate opposite Walnut Tree Farm further along the road. Cross the undulating ground from the gate and make your way towards the church and its south gate. The fact that the church was built on the site of a Norman castle and that a medieval village existed here explains the profile of the ground. The castle keep stood on Toot Hill, the mound near the churchyard's south-west corner. Once in the churchyard turn left (or right for a view of Ivy Cottage) and follow the path through a gate. Pass to the right of the mound, then turn left in the road at the end and left again for the Motte and Bailey pub.

PLACE OF INTEREST NEARBY

Hitchin Museum and Art Gallery. See page 92 (Great Offley) for details.

The Cricketers

THIS WALK STARTS WITH A MINI TOUR OF THE BEST OF THIS DELIGHTFUL VILLAGE – ITS TINY GREEN AND POND, ITS THATCHED HOUSES AND ITS WELL-KEPT COTTAGE TERRACES. IT PASSES THROUGH THE IDYLLIC PRECINCTS OF THE PARISH CHURCH BEFORE CROSSING FIELDS TO HALL'S GREEN, AND RETURNS TO WESTON ACROSS A SERIES OF LUSH GREEN MEADOWS.

THE CRICKETERS offers a warm and friendly welcome to all – including families – where well-cooked, home prepared food is on offer, and where it does not cost the earth! A good selection is available from the regular menu and the daily specials board. Examples are home-made steak and kidney pie, mixed grill and smoked haddock Florentine. A variety of fresh fish is delivered daily, which is good news for many fish lovers. All this every lunchtime and evening except Sunday evening.

For liquid refreshment the Cricketers offers Fuller's London Pride and at least two other guest ales throughout the year. There is a large selection of wines to choose from, by the glass or bottle. During the summer months the pub is open all day on Saturdays and Sundays. At other times it keeps to traditional hours. There is a large garden, with fine views overlooking the open countryside: an ideal place to relax in fine weather, and where children can play in safety.

Large walking parties are always welcome, but it is advisable to book meals or snacks in advance.

✆ 01462 790273.

How to get there: If you are coming via the A1 (M) join the A6141 near Letchworth (in the Baldock direction) and soon turn right into the B197, then first left for Weston. Once at Weston (by the Red Lion) turn right into Damask Green Road for the Cricketers.
Parking: In the pub's car park or along the roadside.
Length of the walk: 3¾ miles. Map: OS Landranger 166 Luton, Hertford and surrounding area (GR 258298).

THE WALK

1 From the Cricketers go left along Damask Green Road to the Red Lion, then straight on along Fore Street, with the green and its pond on your right. About 100 yards before what was once the White Horse pub (which is at a road junction) join a rough drive on the right signposted to Maiden Street. This drive soon runs into a footpath which passes between lovely cottage gardens to a road.

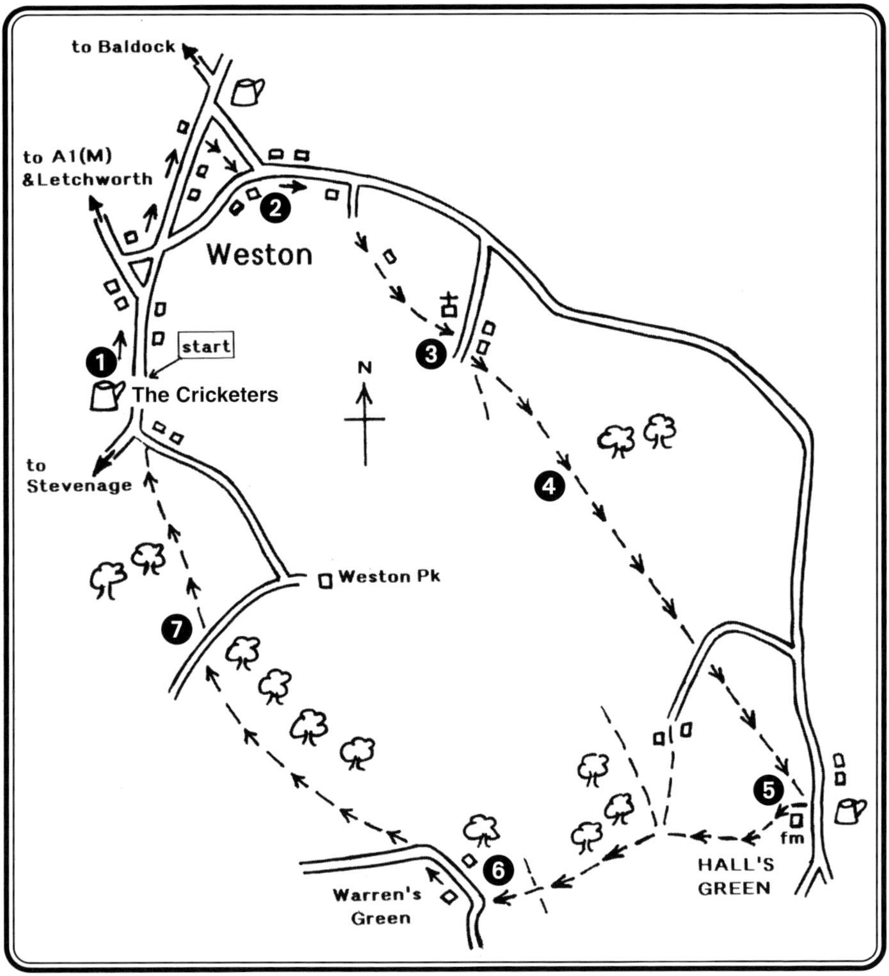

2 Turn left in the road and follow this downhill to where it narrows; then turn right into a drive just beyond a school. When the drive soon terminates continue forward, but now along a footpath between hedges. This passes a pair of almshouses and runs between fields to the churchyard gate.

3 As you leave the churchyard's east gate (straight on) turn right in the church drive and very soon left into a footpath signposted 'Halls Green 1' immediately beyond Glebe Cottage. Follow the cottage hedge for just a few yards before crossing a field straight on (140°) aiming at the right-hand end of a wood ¼ mile ahead. This path will take you into a dip and across a ditch, then slightly right and uphill towards an electricity pole at the top. Looking back see what a fine picture the church and cottages make.

4 Go through a hedge gap by that pole and continue forward, now following overhead wires and about 75 yards to the right of the aforementioned wood, with a hedge on your right. Stay with the wires in and out of another dip and over a drive, then across a field followed by a small pasture. Cross the next field (the last, for the time being) straight on to its corner (without the wires), aiming for the Rising Sun pub sign by the road at Hall's Green.

5 Do not join the road (unless attracted by the Rising Sun) but turn right from the field corner along a wide farm drive, passing to the right of farm buildings. Soon go half-left (diagonally) across the yard to a track leaving from its corner and follow this across fields and alongside trees. Go left with the track from a junction of ways and, with a wood on your immediate right, stay the course for ⅓ mile until you meet the road at Warren's Green.

6 Turn right in the road and go along this to where it turns left. Leave the road here by going forward through a kissing-gate and along the short left edge of a small meadow. When a stile soon places you in a larger meadow you should go slightly left (290°) to pass 20 yards left of an ancient oak tree; then more or less straight on across what turns out to be a series of stiles and meadows, eventually (⅓ mile) walking alongside the wood on the right.

The venerable oak tree passed at point 6 of the walk.

7 Cross a tarmac drive to a kissing-gate and walk the edge of the right-hand field straight on to a kissing-gate in the far left-hand corner, passing close to a wood edge as you go. Turn left in the drive there and soon join Damask Green Road. Turn right back to the Cricketers.

PLACES OF INTEREST NEARBY

Cromer Windmill is situated 3 miles south-east of Weston. Approach via Halls Green (the half-way point of our walk) and the B1037 (GR 305287).

The mill is open every Sunday and Bank Holiday Monday and every second and fourth Saturday from mid-May to mid-September – afternoons only. There is a small entrance charge. Telephone: 01279 849901. The mill is included in website www.hbpt.co.uk

The Rose and Crown

NOT FAR FROM ASHWELL'S MARVELLOUS HIGH STREET, THE WALK JOINS A TRACK HEADING FOR THE SUMMIT OF NEWNHAM HILL, WHERE THERE ARE OUTSTANDING VIEWS ACROSS NEARBY BEDFORDSHIRE AND CAMBRIDGESHIRE. THE WALK DESCENDS TO MEDIEVAL HINXWORTH PLACE AND RETURNS TO ASHWELL ACROSS LEVEL FIELDS AND ALONG QUIET LANES.

THE ROSE AND CROWN, Ashwell's oldest pub, takes full advantage of its prime position in one of Hertfordshire's most attractive villages by the welcome afforded to its customers and by the quality and variety of its food and drink.

A full menu is offered lunchtimes and evenings (except Sunday evenings), including chef's fish specials, a seasonal menu and traditional pub fare. In addition to a roast, the Sunday menu includes a variety of meals from hot dishes through to sandwiches. The large open fireplace will keep you warm in the winter months, while in summer the secluded garden area will be an ideal place to relax after your walk.

Real ales are Greene King IPA, and Abbot Ale. These are supplemented by guest ales, which vary throughout the year. Traditional opening hours are kept, except at weekends when the pub is open all day. There is a separate dining room, which is ideal for families.

Organised walking parties are very welcome, but prior warning of an invasion would be appreciated! Dogs are also welcome.

✆ 01462 742420.

How to get there: Ashwell is signposted from the A505 3 miles north-east of Baldock. Turn left when you reach Ashwell's High Street; the pub will then be on your left.
Parking: In the pub's car park. Roadside parking is possible but limited: try Swan Street nearby, between the High Street and the parish church.
Length of the walk: 5¼ miles. Map: OS Landranger 153 Bedford, Huntingdon and surrounding area (GR 267396).

THE WALK

1 Turning left out of the Rose and Crown you will soon pass Bear House which has an interesting architectural feature: seven quatrefoils in the north-east corner. These acted as ventilators for the food store in this 14th century hall-house.

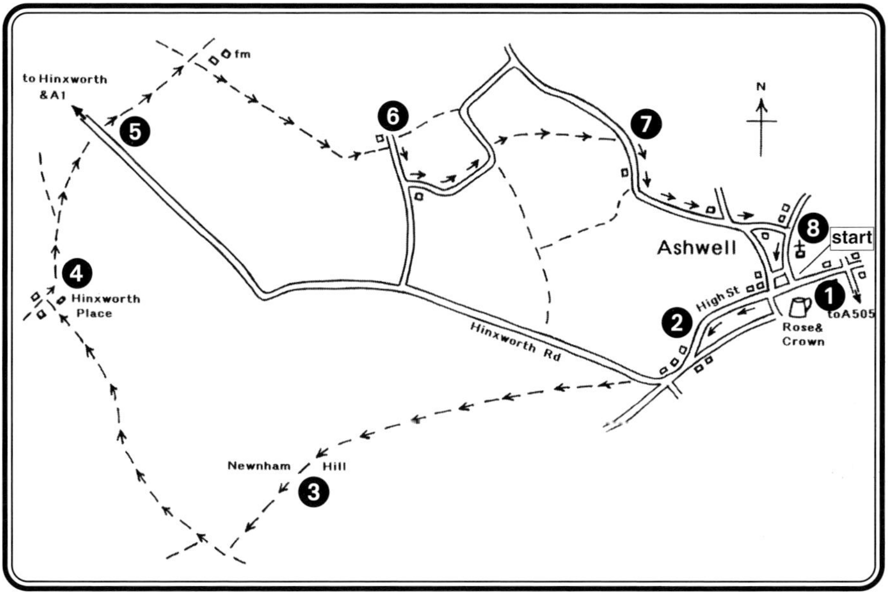

2 Continuing along the High Street you may notice that it becomes West End before describing an S bend. When you meet Hinxworth Road branch right into this and, when it soon curves right, join a chalky track going straight on. After following the backs of gardens you will be launched into open country, with a hedge for company and a magnificent view across Bedfordshire and Cambridgeshire – and a little of Hertfordshire.

3 When the hedge bears left beyond the summit of the track, go with it downhill for ¼ mile to a waymarked T-junction. Turn right here and follow another hedge downhill (300°) in the general direction of a distant water tower. Ignore a path going left when you are almost down to the lowest level and continue forward, with Hinxworth church coming into view directly ahead. By keeping straight on along a series of field edges, you will eventually (⅔ mile) pass between a long black timber barn and a garden. Soon after this a waymark post appears on the right, and a collection of timber cottages directly ahead. A short diversion to the left along a drive will place you close to Hinxworth Place, thought to be one of the best-preserved stone manor houses in Hertfordshire. It was built in the 1400s with chalk stone quarried locally.

4 Return to the waymark post and follow a hedge for 30 yards to another post at a hedge corner. Turn half-left from the hedge corner and pass between a woodland plantation and a very large field (10°). If a tiled-roof barn is directly behind you, you are on course! When you are almost halfway along the field a path might be apparent heading towards Hinxworth church: ignore this and bear half-right to another waymark post in a hedge corner, then straight on again following a hedge of sorts into the field's far left-hand corner, and on to a road.

5 Cross the road to a bridleway opposite (the drive to Arbtree Farm) and go along this for ¼ mile to a concreted area, near barns and about 50 yards before a pole-mounted transformer. Turn right here between the trees (120°), soon entering a field and continuing straight on, aiming at two light grey barns ⅔ mile away. A footbridge on the far side of this field places you on a path in a much smaller field, and this in turn leads you straight on to a narrow hedge gap and footbridge opposite. Go through the gap and into another field and turn left immediately, following the hedge to a lane at the field corner (70°).

6 Turn right in the lane and left at a T-junction, near those grey barns. Passing The Oaks bungalow and farm (near the corner) stay with the lane to its second left bend. Ignore the by-way sign in the corner and continue to the footpath sign on the right just around the corner. Go over the stile here and head half-right across the field, passing about 20 yards

to the right of an electricity pole (60° initially). The path curves right a little as it crosses the field, and heads towards barns (dark grey this time) joining a lane from a stile – a few yards right of a hedge gap. Ashwell's parish church has now come into view.

7 On leaving the field turn right in the lane and go left with it at a turning. Continue forward at a road junction, and forward again into Rollys Lane, where you have a view of Ashwell Bury beyond the pasture on the left. From the end of the lane turn right into Mill Street (or left to see the mill and its wheels, and the river) and pass between the church and the Bushel and Strike pub.

8 The church is certainly worth more than a passing glance. What are referred to as the Graffiti Scratchings can be seen on the inside tower wall. They include a drawing of Old St Paul's before the Great Fire of London in 1666; also inscriptions relating to the Plague of 1349–50 and the Great Storm of 1362.

At the top of Mill Street lies Swan Street and the fine timber-framed building housing Ashwell's museum and, to the right of this, a lovely cottage garden maintained by the villagers, who successfully fought off an attempt to build here. Passing the garden and turning left out of Swan Street into Gardiners Lane, glance back at the unusual chalk wall – complete with thatch.

PLACE OF INTEREST NEARBY

Therfield Heath is 5 miles east of Ashwell off the A505 near Royston. Described as the largest area of flower-rich chalk grassland remaining in Hertfordshire, it is particularly prized for its colony of pasque flowers.

The Chequers

A WALK WITH WIDE SWEEPING VIEWS TYPICAL OF NORTH HERTFORDSHIRE, MELLOWED BY THE WOODLANDS OF NEWSELLS PARK AND THE BEAUTIFULLY KEPT COTTAGES AT SMITH'S END.

THE CHEQUERS is an attractive pub which cannot fail to impress when you approach it for the first time. On entering you will be equally impressed by the welcoming atmosphere and, in winter, also by the warming open fire. This can be enjoyed all day over the long weekends of Friday to Sunday. On the remaining days the pub is open at the traditional hours (i.e. twice daily) except perhaps in summer when it may be open all day.

Food is available lunchtimes and evenings except Sunday evenings. Examples of meals offered are beef and ale pie, sausage and mash, and a range of filled baguettes. Among the pub's specialities are fish and vegetarian dishes, goat's cheese and spinach parcels and (in season) breast of pheasant. Roasts are available on Sundays, alongside a choice of other traditional meals.

The regular beer is Greene King IPA. Other beers that make an appearance include Old Speckled Hen, Abbot Ale, Fireside and XX Mild.

Families are welcome; and children may choose from their own menu or have smaller adult meals. Dogs are also welcome but owners should check with the landlord before taking them inside.

✆ 01763 848378.

How to get there: The pub is at the top of London Road (the B1368) near The Mount. Barley can be approached from Royston along the B1039 followed by the B1368 (3 miles).
Parking: In the pub's car park or in The Mount, a side road behind the pub.
Length of the walk: 3½ miles. Map: OS Landranger 154 Cambridge, Newmarket and surrounding area (GR 396382).

THE WALK

1 The walk starts from The Mount, which is a short road behind the Chequers. To access this, go sharp right out of the pub and cross the car park; then turn left where a

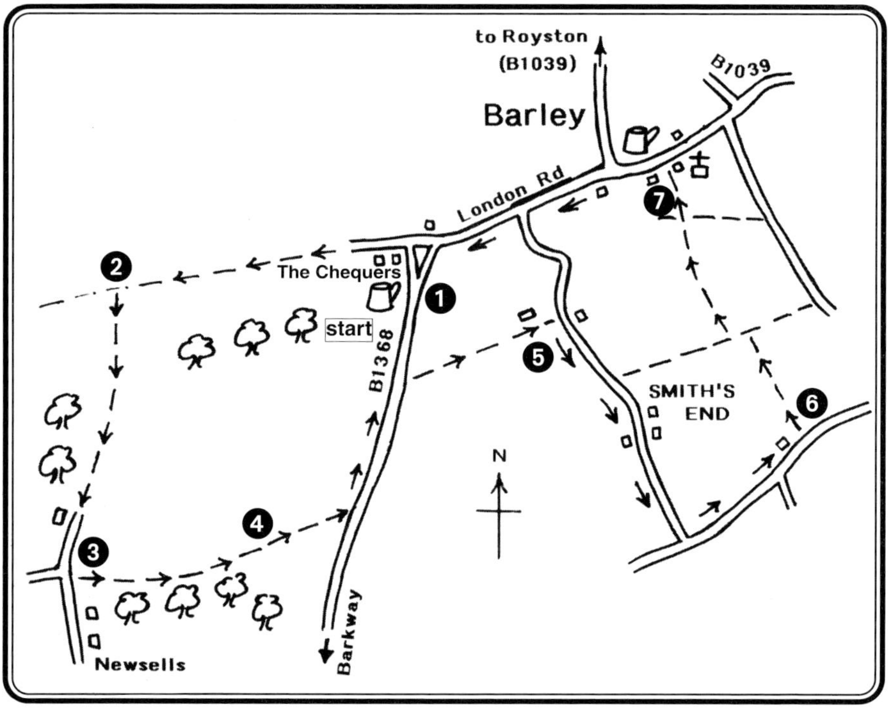

cottage occupies a corner at a T-junction. This branch evolves into a track and takes you downhill to the bottom of a wide valley. Turn left there into a sandy track with a 'Private' notice now behind you and paddocks on your right.

2 After you cross a very superior drive and continue straight on, you will pass between hedges along a more conventional track. The track becomes a road by Fox Cottage and joins a three-way road junction. Your next move is to climb the bank to the left of a rough-hewn memorial stone but, if you take delight in old thatched cottages, there are four immaculate specimens to be seen along the road ahead. These are within the approaches to Newsells Park, a house

burnt down in the Second World War and rebuilt in Georgian style in 1954.

3 Having climbed that bank in the direction of the signpost finger (90°), you will soon be walking just inside a wood. The path comes briefly out into the open at the top of the hill, giving an equally brief view over the paddocks. It crosses a drive here and resumes its passage under the trees. When you come out into the open at the bottom of the hill go forward a few yards to a gate.

4 The next stage is to go straight on to a road directly ahead. For this you should pass between paddocks and through a plantation; then cross a drive to the road. Turn left in the road and follow this down to a footpath sign on the right, where the road begins to ascend. Cross the ditch here (planks are provided) and strike across the field towards its summit (65°), eventually meeting up with a terrace of three cottages. You may well find that the path is obliterated by crops. If this is the case you should if possible keep to the prescribed route – and have the satisfaction of helping those who follow.

5 From the cottages pass to the left of a black metal barn and join a road. You could now call it a day by turning left here for Barley (⅓ mile), but in so doing you will miss the delightful hamlet of Smith's End, as well as some good views thereafter. Assuming you are persuaded, turn right and walk through the hamlet (⅓ mile) to a T-junction in the road. Turn left there (Nuthampstead direction) and go downhill to a track on the left signposted 'Barley ½' 60 yards beyond the next road junction.

6 When this uphill track goes left to a paddock, continue forward along a footpath, following power lines and enjoying the view – which includes Chishill's windmill

¾ mile over to your right. And, when confronted by a hedge at a T-junction in the path, turn left and go through a kissing-gate in the hedge after a few yards. Then resume your previous direction by crossing a pasture and aiming (to the left of a hedge) for a wooden electricity pole where wires branch three ways. Go through a kissing-gate just beyond the pole and keep forward between hedges, ignoring a kissing-gate on the right and continuing in the main path straight on to Church End, Barley.

7 Across the road from the church is the very fine Tudor Town House built in about 1530; it is now the village hall. It has a varied history, including (or so it is said) courthouse, workhouse, almshouse and school. At the road junction opposite the Fox and Hounds the 17th century lock up or cage was used for the temporary detention of suspected lawbreakers and drunks – very conveniently placed for the pub!

Having passed the Fox and Hounds, go forward into London Road – in the Barkway and Hare Street direction – and follow this uphill to the Chequers pub.

PLACE OF INTEREST NEARBY

The site of **Nuthampstead's wartime airfield** is 2½ miles south of Barley. In the Second World War it was the base of the 398th Bomb Group, US Air Force. A memorial to the group can be seen outside the Woodman public house in Nuthampstead village. From Barley take the B1368 south to Barkway and turn left just beyond the Tally Ho public house (GR 413345).